MY JAMAICAN TABLE

MY JAMAICAN TABLE

VIBRANT RECIPES *from a* SUN-DRENCHED ISLAND

ANDRE FOWLES

Foreword by
Bruce Springsteen

ARTISAN | NEW YORK

Library of Congress Cataloging-in-Publication Data

Names: Fowles, Andre author | Springsteen, Bruce writer of foreword
Title: My Jamaican table / Andre Fowles ; foreword by Bruce Springsteen.
Description: New York : Artisan, [2026] | Includes index.
Identifiers: LCCN 2025026567 | ISBN 9781648293740 hardback
Subjects: LCSH: Cooking, Jamaican | LCGFT: Cookbooks
Classification: LCC TX716.J27 F695 2026 | DDC 641.597292—dc23/eng/20250702
LC record available at https://lccn.loc.gov/2025026567

ISBN 978-1-64829-374-0
ISBN 978-1-64829-565-2 (signed edition)
ISBN 978-1-64829-400-6 (ebook)

Design by Becky Terhune

Published by Artisan
an imprint of Workman Publishing,
a division of Hachette Book Group, Inc.
1290 Avenue of the Americas
New York, NY 10104
artisanbooks.com

Printed in China (APO) on responsibly sourced paper

First printing, January 2026

1 3 5 7 9 10 8 6 4 2

CONTENTS

ROLEX

FOREWORD

by Bruce Springsteen

I first met Andre a few years ago through a good friend of mine. At the time, Patti and I had no idea a simple introduction would lead to a friendship that now feels like family. My friend had been telling us about this young Jamaican chef with a knack for capturing the soul of the island in every dish, and after our first meal together, I knew we had something special.

Andre isn't just a chef. He's an artist. There's a sense of history, place, and heart in everything he puts on a plate. When you sit down for a meal cooked by Andre, you're not just eating—you're experiencing something deeper. And let me tell you, it's real. The flavors hit you like the opening chords of a song you didn't know you needed to hear, but once you do, you can't imagine your life without it.

Now, I've been around plenty of talented people in my lifetime, but what sets Andre apart are his humility and his love for what he does. You'd never guess he's a three-time *Chopped* champion because he's so down-to-earth. Andre brings this same grounded spirit to all his efforts, whether he's cooking for family, friends, or folks he just met. Patti and I are lucky enough to know him both in and out of the kitchen, and he's got that rare gift of making you feel like you're part of his world.

This cookbook reflects that gift. It's not just recipes—it's a window into Andre's journey, his heritage, and his deep connection to Jamaica. You'll find classic dishes you've heard about, like jerk chicken and rice and peas, but you'll also discover flavors and combinations that'll surprise you—things you'll want to bring into your own kitchen, even if you've never been to Jamaica. This book is going to change the way you think about Caribbean cooking.

When Andre cooks, there's joy in it—joy in the spices, in the sizzle of the pan, in the balance of heat and sweetness. And what I love most is that his food is made for sharing. I think that's why we hit it off so well. We both believe in bringing people together, whether it's around a table or a stage.

I couldn't be prouder to write this foreword for my friend. I've seen firsthand the dedication, the craft, and the passion that Andre pours into his work. This cookbook is the culmination of years of experience, but it's also a love letter to the food and people of Jamaica. You're in good hands. So grab your spices, fire up the grill, and let Andre show you how it's done.

PREFACE

I've always believed food is more than just what's on the plate—it's a story, a connection, and a legacy. Growing up in Kingston, Jamaica, I was surrounded by bold flavors, proud traditions, and a deep love for the island's culture. Cooking became my way of expressing that love, whether in my grandmother's kitchen or, later, on international stages.

Jamaican food is the soul of the island. It tells the story of our people, and of taking the hardships of our past and turning them into something beautiful and delicious. I want to bring the flavors of Jamaica to your kitchen, whether you're a seasoned cook or someone just discovering our food. This book is for you if you crank up the reggae to stay connected to the island. It's for you if you live too far away from your favorite cookshop. It's for you even if you've never been to Jamaica.

Over the years, I've had the privilege of representing Jamaica on global platforms, including winning Food Network's *Chopped* three times. Those victories weren't just for me; they were also for Jamaica. It's been my honor to take the flavors of my home and show the world what makes our food, and our people, so special. I've cooked for dignitaries, celebrities, and food lovers all over, but my heart always comes back to Jamaica. This cookbook is the culmination of that journey—a love letter to Jamaica, her people, and her food.

TOYOTA
5603 KG

INTRODUCTION

Dappled sunlight flickering through the trees. A tendril of smoke unfurling from the coal fire. The perfume of red peas rising from coconut milk in a well-worn pot. I can almost taste the thyme and Scotch bonnet. It's like I've returned to my grandmother's kitchen. These are the sights, tastes, and smells that bring me to Jamaica.

Jamaican cuisine is the result of a rich blend of cultural influences: Indigenous, African, Indian, Chinese, and European. Each culinary thread brings its own flavors and techniques, yielding foods that are diverse and deeply rooted in the past. From the fiery spices of African heritage to the aromatic herbs of Indian cuisine, every dish tells a story of resilience and adaptation. This fusion defines not only our culinary identity but the spirit of Jamaica itself—dynamic, colorful, and always evolving.

Iconic Jamaican foods like jerk pork, peppered shrimp, and ackee and saltfish tell the stories of the island's culture and history. Essential herbs and spices elevate them, creating layers of complexity that define Jamaican cuisine. As with most cooking, fresh ingredients are key, but with Jamaican dishes those especially include herbs like thyme, green onion—referred to as scallions in Jamaica and in the recipes—and garlic.

To me, Jamaican food is always about maximum flavor, and we go above and beyond to inject as much as possible. We soak beans, cook them slowly, and use aromatics at every step. We layer heat and sweet and savory. We marinate meats for hours to let the seasonings and spices fully penetrate. If you plan ahead and take your time, the results will be well worth it.

My Jamaican Table is a culinary journey through the heart and soul of Jamaica. It's a collection of the flavors and memories that have shaped my life. It was inspired by my grandmother's kitchen, where the scents of garlic and ginger were infused with laughter, love, and more than a few hard times.

MY STORY: NOT AN EASY ROAD

I grew up on the rough streets of downtown Kingston, where, along with playing games, we learned how to survive and even thrive. It was there, surrounded by family and community, that I discovered food as a bridge to hope.

Our home was in a tenement yard on George's Lane. We had a tiny area for cooking, space for a table, and a bedroom I occupied with three siblings. We shared a small yard, a washroom, and a shower with other tenants on the property, all of whom were just like us: struggling to get by.

My mom, Patsy, cooked and sold breakfast to make ends meet. Each morning, she left home at 4 a.m. to go to the market to buy whatever she could get at a good price: callaloo, sweet potato—whatever was cheap that day—plus ackee, because it was on the menu every day. Shopping done, she took her supplies to a tiny, makeshift, hole-in-the-wall cookshop and got to work. When I didn't have school, I helped prepare the ackee; this was my first exposure to working in the kitchen.

I was ten when my mother left us. One day I came home from school and my grandmother, Mama Cherry, was making dinner and singing along to reggae hits on the radio. That evening she told us our mother had gone to England to work. My mom called us early the next morning to explain everything. She would only be gone a year, she said.

Mama Cherry took over the care and feeding of me and my siblings. My mom sent money whenever she could, and it was more than what she'd been making in Jamaica, so things felt a bit easier. We could afford what we needed for school, and we ate more complete meals. It was, for me, the first glimmer of hope that this life could be a little better.

We were all sure that once you made it off the island and went to "farrin" (foreign), your life would change. A lot of us grew up like that. If your parent got a chance to go abroad, they did. Some forgot they had kids. Thankfully my mom wasn't one of those, but seventeen years passed before she returned to Jamaica.

My culinary journey continued in the kitchen standing next to Mama Cherry. From her, I learned much more than chopping, stirring, and tasting—I learned about love, responsibility, and perseverance. My decision to go to culinary school was more about survival than anything else. I wanted

to be a pediatrician, but I knew from early on there was no chance I would be able to study medicine. My mom was struggling to make ends meet in England, and the money she sent for me and my siblings barely stretched. I knew I'd have to help her provide for the family, or at least be able to support myself soon. I was twelve.

When I looked at my options, cooking seemed the quickest route to a job, so in my second year of high school, I started the food and nutrition program with Miss Campbell. She was a tough, no-nonsense disciplinarian who held us to high standards, but if you worked hard and did well, she was very kind to you. She must have seen something in me from the beginning because she pushed me, and instead of pushing back, I excelled. I loved food. I loved the creativity, theory, philosophy, and history of cooking. Being in the kitchen came naturally to me.

By the time I finished high school, the HEART Trust Academy in Kingston—the local trade school—was getting popular. I'd heard stories about graduates getting jobs in hotels and even overseas right out of school. The local TV station had programs featuring graduate chefs working at resorts around the country, and I wanted that. I applied and got in. Level 1—the basic program—took six months to complete and I graduated at the top of the class.

I got a job right away with a catering company in Kingston. On my first night we worked at a large outdoor carnival party. I arrived well before start time to set up. Within a few hours, thousands of people were gyrating and grinding and sweating under a starry midnight sky. Live soca music blasted across the crowd, pounding in my chest. The sharp, sweet aroma of jerk chicken wafted overhead. I washed glasses at a plastic sink for ten hours. The more I washed, the more the glasses piled up. I was sixteen.

The next year, I was offered a position at what was arguably the best restaurant in Jamaica at the time, Mac's Chop House. I had two weeks to learn all eighteen menu items at the pastry and cold appetizer station. It took me a week and suddenly I was the chef garde manger, fully responsible for the desserts and foods from the cold side of the kitchen line—things like salads, appetizers, pâtés, and other cold foods. This was my introduction to fine dining.

About two years into this job, I was ready for more challenges and more training. I was accepted to the Culinary Institute of America program offered through HEART. For the next four years I held a full-time job with the caterer *and* on Saturdays I rode a bus three hours each way to attend classes. I loved it. Not the bus ride, the classes. It was exhausting, but I stayed focused and did well. I did so well that the head of the program told the board of the Culinary Federation of Jamaica about me, and that was how I was offered a job at the prestigious Round Hill Resort on Jamaica's north coast with chef Martin Maginley. I hadn't yet finished school, but I wanted to be exposed to a higher level of culinary excellence, and I would find that at Round Hill.

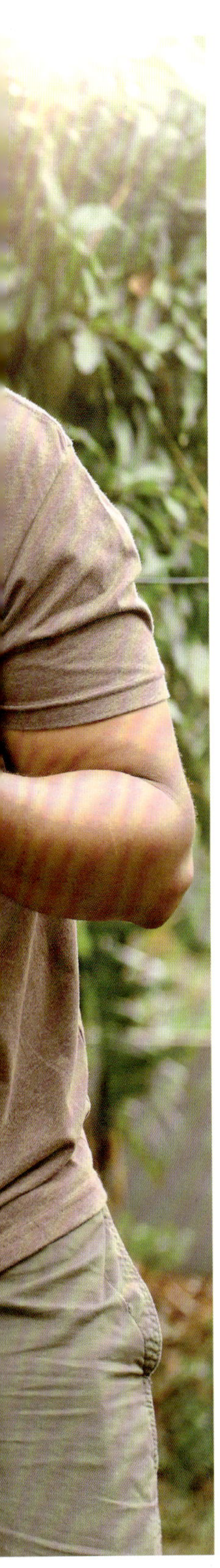

I was promoted to chef de partie within my first year at the Round Hill Resort. My fellow chefs called me the utility knife of the kitchen because I could work any station. If there was a private client in one of the villas, I could handle it—cook a great meal, carry myself well, and not lose my head if they were famous. I was personable, fast, and energetic, and I was quickly promoted to sous-chef. I stayed in that position for four years.

In time, I wanted to get out of Jamaica to find better opportunities. A dear friend and mentor, Susan Couch, introduced me to Paul Salmon, who owns Skylark and Rockhouse Hotel in Negril, Jamaica, and Miss Lily's, a popular Jamaican restaurant in New York. I'll always be grateful to Susan, who is no longer with us, for that introduction—it set so much in motion. Paul hired me to work at the original Miss Lily's location and to help open a second one, so for a while it felt like I was working seven days a week.

Within six months the second Miss Lily's was up and running, and a year later, someone at work handed me a card with a name and *Chopped* on it. "The guy said you should apply to get on the show," she said. I couldn't believe what I was hearing. I applied, and two months later I was competing. I won (three times, in fact), and it changed everything. Miss Lily's got really busy after that.

I was eventually able to buy Mama Cherry a new house in Jamaica. I loved being able to do that for her. And no matter how far from home I traveled or how much time passed, she was always there, a constant source of wisdom and love. I called her often and visited her whenever money allowed. One morning a few years later I got a call from Jamaica I'd been dreading. Mama Cherry had been diagnosed with stomach cancer a few months earlier, and the treatment hadn't helped. I arrived from New York that evening and was able to be with her in her final moments.

This sacred time with my beloved Mama Cherry softened me, broke me a little, and made me a stronger, more tender version of myself. It's clear to me now that the hours we spent together in the kitchen weren't just about food; they were about love and family and showing up for the people who matter.

My Jamaican Table is for Mama Cherry, but it's also a love letter to Jamaica's incredible spirit, her people, and her rich traditions. It is a celebration of our proud, resilient little country. The recipes capture flavors that have been passed down to me through generations, infused with the stories and experiences that make our island one of a kind.

Through these pages, I want to introduce Jamaica to those who have never visited or don't know much about our culture. I want to share a slice of our history and bring the essence of Jamaica into your home.

HOW TO USE THIS BOOK

Jamaican cooking shouldn't be intimidating. This book is here to guide you, with tips on finding ingredients, using easy substitutions, and adapting flavors to what you have on hand. With a little creativity and some basic ingredients, you'll be able to capture the essence of Jamaican cuisine in your own kitchen. The recipes are approachable but authentic, meant for cooks at any skill level.

As a chef, I prefer to make fresh stock (chicken, beef, vegetable, etc.), but most home cooks don't have the time or resources for this. In Jamaica, people use Maggi or Grace bouillon cubes. You could also use a bouillon paste; my preference is Better Than Bouillon.

Throughout this cookbook, you'll see measurements given in both U.S. standard measures and metrics, with metric units rounded for simplicity. For liquids, a standard U.S. cup holds 240 milliliters, but most measuring cups are marked in 25-milliliter increments, so for simplicity, I've rounded up to 250 milliliters. The differences are minor and won't affect the outcome of the recipes, especially if you're using the same measuring cup consistently throughout. In most cases, an extra 10 milliliters of liquid (or even more or less) won't make or break any dish.

Your regular pots and pans are all you need. When I say "skillet," I mean a stainless steel or cast-iron frying pan. I recognize that a lot of people—including me—don't have a barbecue grill, so I've included options for using your oven for recipes that call for grilling. I don't have a fancy kitchen, and you don't need one either to make any of these recipes.

One of my early mentors, chef Kenrick Stewart, always said, "Recipes are meant to be a guide, not a shackle." I hope you embrace this spirit while cooking from this book. Feel free to make these recipes your own—tweak, experiment, and adjust to suit your taste.

The recipes begin with a chapter that invites you to dive in hands-first with Jamaica's favorite finger foods. From savory Jamaican Beef Patties (page 40) to the thoroughly addictive Jerk Street Corn (page 55), these dishes are meant to be enjoyed with no utensils—just a hearty appetite!

The following chapters mix Jamaican classics like Rice and Peas (page 127) with modern twists, including dishes like Coffee-Cocoa Lamb Chops (page 226) and Sweet Jerk Crispy Cauliflower (page 156). Throughout, you'll find recipes that feature some of my favorite Jamaican flavors—allspice and thyme, for example. They show up in dishes like Ital-Style Red Peas Soup (page 105), Oxtail and Butter Beans (page 163), and even desserts and drinks.

At the end of the book, Starting from Scratch offers core recipes for seasonings and sauces used throughout the recipes, with ideas for introducing them in your own dishes.

This book is my tribute to a way of life where meals are shared, stories told, and bonds strengthened. I want it to exist in the world not for myself, because I cook these dishes all the time, but for the people of Jamaica. Our food expresses who we are and what we've been through, and I want this book to help the world understand that. I want people to know why we cook the way we do, and who we are as a nation.

Finally, this book is an homage to the strong women in my life. I hope that as you read the stories and look at the photos, you feel the spirit of our people: proud, kind, strong, and resilient. That's my Jamaica.

SALTFISH
$600
½ 300
CHOICE BLOATERS 61-80
CAP-PELE HERRING
EXPORT INC.
CAP-PELE, NB E4N 1C2
PRODUCT OF CANADA
CLOVES
Dandelion
Powder
BETTY
mac & cheese
SEAFOOD FROM NORWAY

MY JAMAICAN PANTRY

In my Jamaican pantry, each ingredient tells a story. Some of them are essentials and form the backbone of our cuisine, and others are my personal favorites. Divided into four main sections—produce, proteins, seasonings, and staples—this guide is your go-to for stocking a kitchen that's ready to bring vibrant, authentic Jamaican flavors to life.

From the familiar heat of Scotch bonnet peppers and the warmth of pimento (our beloved allspice) to lesser-known ingredients like cho-cho (chayote) and saltfish, each item brings its own depth. There are staples you won't want to skip and optional extras that add a unique twist. The Resources section (page 320) lists my favorite brands of some of the ingredients found in the recipes as well as suggestions for where to find them. I've also included tips on substitutions, so you can still capture the essence of these dishes no matter where you're cooking.

PRODUCE

ACKEE: Ackee is a voluptuous tropical fruit native to West Africa and closely related to the lychee. Known for its buttery texture and mild, nutty flavor, ackee becomes orangey-red and opens naturally when ripe. When cooked properly, its tender, creamy flesh pairs deliciously with salt cod in Jamaica's national dish, Ackee and Saltfish (page 78), and looks a little bit like scrambled eggs. Canned ackee is now available throughout North America and Europe and is the recommended option unless you know how to prepare ackee fresh.

BREADFRUIT: Roasted, fried, or made into chips, breadfruit is a starchy fruit with a texture similar to that of bread but is used more like a potato. Breadfruit was brought to Jamaica by Captain William Bligh in the eighteenth century to feed people enslaved on plantations. At home, the preferred way to cook breadfruit is to roast it directly in charcoal embers in a coal pot until the outside is black and the inside is steamed to soft, doughy perfection. You can also roast it in the oven, then peel, slice, and fry it in a pan with butter.

CALLALOO: This leafy green is often added to soups or served as a side dish on its own, sautéed with onions, garlic, and tomatoes (see page 81). You can find fresh or frozen callaloo in most Afro-Caribbean markets and canned callaloo in the international aisle of many supermarkets. If you can't find callaloo, you can substitute fresh spinach, kale, or Swiss chard.

CASSAVA: Also known as yuca or manioc, this starchy root vegetable is the underground part of the cassava shrub. It's a drought-resistant crop grown in more than eighty countries, providing a dietary staple for over 800 million people worldwide. It is often boiled or fried, but Jamaicans like to make it into Bammy (page 151).

CHAYOTE: Known as cho-cho in Jamaica (not to be confused with the chocho bean from Ecuador), this mild squash is great in soups and stews, adding texture and nutrients. Every part of the chayote can be eaten, including seeds, flesh, and skin. I prefer to peel it, but you can leave the skin on if you wish. Raw chayote is great in slaws and salads. If you can't find chayote, you can substitute zucchini in a pinch.

GINGER: Ginger is a staple in Jamaican cooking, but it also has a long history in traditional Jamaican medicine for its anti-inflammatory and digestive benefits. In cooking, fresh ginger root is used for its spicy and aromatic qualities. It's essential in many recipes, including marinades, sauces, and drinks like ginger beer.

GREEN BANANAS: Boiled green bananas, a popular side dish, are similar in texture to potatoes. They're often served with breakfast as a side or added to soups like Mannish Water (page 114).

GREEN ONIONS: Green onions are known as scallions in Jamaica and have a mild onion flavor. They are used in soups and stews and make up the base of Green Seasoning (page 308), a popular marinade for meats.

MANGOES: Mangoes are beloved in Jamaica. They go into everything from smoothies to chutneys, or, best of all, they are eaten fresh off the tree. There are several varieties, each with a unique flavor and texture. Fresh, ripe mangoes are best for Mango Salsa (page 217), but frozen mangoes are perfectly fine for Mango Chutney (page 318).

OKRA: This fuzzy green vegetable is the immature seedpod of the okra plant, which grows well in hot, humid climates. It releases a type of sugar that gets slimy when it comes in contact with water. This substance, known as mucilage (not a very selling term, is it?), is what gives soups like Fish Tea (page 113) and stews body and a subtle viscosity. If you're not a fan of this texture, skip the okra in the soup recipes, but please try the Crispy Okra with Scotch Bonnet Mayo (page 58)—that same sugar also dehydrates and makes the okra crunchy in this dish. It's so good, you won't notice anything but the incredible taste.

PLANTAIN: You can tell plantains apart from bananas by their pointy ends, larger size, and starchy texture. Green plantains are more savory and are perfect for Pressed Green Plantain (page 133), while ripe plantains are sweeter and taste great in Plantain and Black Bean Salad (page 155). To pronounce *plantain* properly, say it with "in" at the end, like *mountain* or *fountain*.

PUMPKIN: Jamaican pumpkin, known for its sweetness and vibrant color, is a frequent ingredient in soups and stews. You can find it in stores under the name "calabaza squash," or substitute your favorite hearty squash (like butternut or acorn).

SCOTCH BONNET PEPPERS: These chile peppers are essential for giving a dish authentic Jamaican heat. They come in a variety of colors, each with its own flavor profile. Green Scotch bonnets are fresh and earthy, and their heat is the least potent; yellow and orange peppers bring a bit more heat, along with fruity notes of citrus. The red ones are the hottest and have the most pronounced fruity flavor. When working with Scotch bonnet peppers, start with a small amount and gradually add more to find the level of heat that works for you. Remember, it's all about enhancing the dish without overwhelming (or burning out your taste buds!). If you can't find Scotch bonnet peppers, habanero peppers are a close match, or you can use Scotch Bonnet Sauce (page 310). For a milder option, use a combination of jalapeños and a pinch of cayenne pepper.

SORREL (HIBISCUS): Sorrel is the key ingredient in a gorgeous ruby-red holiday drink (page 300) that's often spiced with ginger and infused with rum. Dried hibiscus is more readily available, but if you have access to fresh hibiscus, give it a try.

SWEET POTATOES: There are about eight thousand varieties of sweet potato around the world. In Jamaica, the most important kind (which you'll need for these recipes) have red skin and white flesh. You may find them labeled as "boniato," "batata," or "Japanese sweet potato" in North America. They are drier and more firm than the darker-fleshed varieties and are used in both savory dishes, like Sweet Potato Salad (page 143), and desserts, like Patsy's Sweet Potato Pudding (page 234).

TAMARIND: Tamarind is a legume that grows in pods on beautiful flowering trees all over Jamaica. The fruit has a tangy, sweet-tart flavor perfect for sauces, including Tamarind Chutney (page 52), as well as drinks and candies. You can find it in the international section of most supermarkets, typically as a paste.

THYME: Fresh thyme is a staple in Jamaican cooking and is often added to soups, stews, and marinades for its earthy, slightly minty flavor and strong aromatic qualities. It's used in everything from jerk marinades to Rice and Peas (page 127).

TURMERIC: Turmeric grows wild in the Cockpit Country of Jamaica and is special for its bright golden color, strong flavor, and high curcumin content. Turmeric powder is a core component of Jamaican curry powder. It gives dishes a vibrant yellow color and a slightly bitter, earthy flavor. Turmeric is also known for its anti-inflammatory properties and has been used for medicinal purposes for thousands of years.

Pimento

Nutmeg

Scotch bonnet

Yam

Coconut

Breadfruit

Plantain

Ackee

YAM: Yam in Jamaica is not the same thing most North American stores sell as yam, which is actually sweet potato. Yam is a starchy root vegetable with rough brown skin on the outside and white or yellow starchy flesh on the inside. It's generally boiled, roasted, or added to soup, especially on Soup Saturdays (see page 101) in Jamaica. Unless you're in an African or Caribbean supermarket, the thing in your cart that looks like a sweet potato almost certainly is a sweet potato and not a yam. The two are not interchangeable in these recipes.

PROTEINS

GOAT MEAT: Introduced to Jamaica by Indian immigrants, goat meat is the main ingredient in Curry Goat (page 170) and Mannish Water (page 114). Both are favorites at Jamaican gatherings and celebrations. If you can't find goat meat, lamb stew meat is an excellent substitute. It has a similar texture and a rich flavor that works well in soups and stews.

OXTAIL: Once considered a lesser cut of meat, oxtail is a much-loved protein in Jamaican cuisine. It's especially good in rich, hearty stews that are cooked for hours over low heat until the meat is falling-off-the-bone tender and the flavors are layered with depth.

PIG'S TAIL: Pig's tail is part of the nose-to-tail culture in Jamaica. We are a people who don't waste anything if we can find a use for it. Cured pig's tail is a great way to intensify the flavor of any dish and can be found in any ethnic supermarket.

SALTED MACKEREL: Mackerel is a fish you see in every supermarket in Jamaica: It comes tinned in brine, tomato sauce, or even hot tomato sauce. It also comes whole, dried, or preserved in salt—this last one is the one you need for these recipes. Mackerel is an inexpensive protein Jamaicans have learned to make into delicious dishes like Mackerel Rundown (page 82), where it's cooked in coconut milk with onions, tomatoes, and spices.

SALTFISH (SALT COD): Saltfish was introduced to Jamaica by European traders and has become a staple in dishes like Ackee and Saltfish (page 78), the national dish of Jamaica, and Saltfish Fritters with Curry Mayo (page 44). Saltfish quality can vary dramatically, and preparing it for use in a recipe takes some advance planning (see How to Prepare Salt Cod, page 46).

SEASONINGS

ALL-PURPOSE SEASONING: This seasoning blend is a kitchen staple in many Jamaican homes, providing a quick and easy way to flavor dishes. Most Jamaicans buy Maggi Season-up! all-purpose seasoning, but I always keep a jar of my homemade blend (page 314) in my pantry.

ALLSPICE: This spice, also known as pimento, is indigenous to Jamaica and was named for its complex flavor profile, which is reminiscent of cinnamon, nutmeg, and clove. It's a key component of jerk seasoning and is used often in Jamaican cooking in general. You can use either whole or ground allspice. If using whole allspice, double the amount of ground allspice a recipe calls for, and be sure to pluck the berries out when you're finished cooking. In a pinch, you can substitute a mixture of equal parts cinnamon, nutmeg, and cloves.

ANNATTO SEED/POWDER: Annatto, also known as achiote, is used primarily for its vibrant color. It has a mild, uniquely earthy flavor and is used to give the crust in Jamaican Beef Patties (page 40) its red hue, as well as supplying the orange shade of the surprisingly delicious canned Tastee Cheese that Jamaicans love to eat with Spice Bun (page 245).

CINNAMON: Cinnamon appears in both sweet and savory dishes in Jamaica to add warmth and depth. Jamaicans love to put it in porridge (page 73) and in many desserts.

CLOVES: Cloves are often used in baking and in beverages like Sorrel (page 300) and are a key ingredient in Christmas Pudding (page 248). Their pungent aroma goes well in savory dishes too, but use them sparingly, as the flavor can take over.

DRY JERK RUB: There are plenty of great store-bought jerk marinades, but making a dry jerk rub from scratch is easy (page 317). It allows you to emphasize some ingredients (or reduce a flavor you're less fond of) and adjust the heat to suit your taste buds. Some people like their jerk to be more allspice-forward and some want it extra hot. Whatever your heat preference, key ingredients include allspice, thyme, and dried Scotch bonnet pepper.

GREEN SEASONING: This blend of fresh herbs and aromatics is a Caribbean staple (each island has its own variation) used for marinating meats and adding flavor to soups and stews. A spoonful of homemade Green Seasoning (page 308) will take any dish up a notch.

JAMAICAN CURRY POWDER: Most commercially available Jamaican curry powder is milder than store-bought Indian curry powder. Ours is a unique blend that reflects the island's culinary fusion and typically includes more turmeric, along with coriander, cumin, fenugreek, and sometimes nutmeg. It's essential for making Jamaican Curry Goat (page 170), Curry Chicken (page 169), and Almost Ital Curry Vegetable Stew (page 175). My favorite brand is Betapac, but Grace and Cool Runnings are also good.

NUTMEG: Nutmeg is the seed of the *Myristica fragrans* tree, indigenous to Indonesia but grown throughout the Caribbean, including Jamaica. Best when grated fresh, nutmeg adds a warm, sweet, and slightly nutty flavor and is great in both sweet and savory dishes.

PAPRIKA: While it's not a traditional Jamaican spice, a lot of Caribbean people use sweet paprika to add color and a mild, sweet flavor to a variety of savory dishes.

SALT: Not all salts are created equal—some are saltier than others. I use and recommend Diamond Crystal kosher salt, which has a light, flaky texture and a milder salinity by volume. If you're using another type, especially table salt or a different brand of kosher salt, use less and adjust to taste.

SOUP MIX: Most soups in Jamaica aren't complete without a packet of Grace Cock Soup Mix, which adds a rich umami flavor and can be found in the international aisle of many supermarkets. You can also make a batch of homemade Soup Seasoning (page 311) to brighten all your soups.

STAPLES

BEANS: You will always find red kidney beans—we call them peas—in a Jamaican kitchen. They are essential for dishes like Ital-Style Red Peas Soup (page 105), Rice and Peas (page 127), and Stew Peas with Pig's Tail (page 165). Gungo peas (pigeon peas) are often used during the Christmas season in rice and soup. For all the recipes in this book, you can use either canned beans or dried beans that have been rehydrated and cooked until tender. I prefer dried beans soaked overnight, which bring a nice color and texture you can't get from canned beans. Dried beans will generally give a richer, more complex flavor than canned beans and hold their shape better during cooking. The longer cooking process with dried beans also means they will be better able to absorb the flavors of broth and spices. Canned beans are more expensive but will save a lot of time, so ultimately the decision comes down to your priorities: convenience versus superior taste and texture. The recipes here include instructions for both canned and dried kidney beans.

BROWNING: This caramelized sauce is made from burnt sugar and is used to add color and depth to stews and gravies like Brown Stew Chicken (page 178) and Oxtail and Butter Beans (page 163).

COCONUT MILK: Coconut milk adds fat, flavor, and richness to dishes like rice and peas, curries, soups, breads, and desserts. The smooth, slightly sweet taste balances bold spices and enhances the overall depth of flavor in traditional recipes. I use canned coconut milk because it's more convenient, but my grandmother used to make her own coconut milk, and you can too (see page 107).

CONDENSED MILK: Sweetened condensed milk is a much-loved ingredient in Jamaica and a common addition to breakfast porridge (page 73), desserts, and drinks, including Guinness Punch (page 298). If you have a little left over in the can, it's great for jazzing up your coffee.

CORNMEAL: Fine yellow cornmeal is used for making dishes like Cornmeal Porridge (page 73), a traditional Jamaican breakfast, and Jamaican Festival (page 137), which is fried dumplings often served with jerk chicken.

HOMINY CORN: Hominy corn is dried corn kernels that have been soaked in an alkaline solution, a process called nixtamalization. This process softens the hulls, giving the kernels a puffy, slightly chewy texture, and makes nutrients like vitamin B3 more accessible for our bodies to absorb. Corn has been grown in Jamaica since the Taino arrived around 800 CE, and Jamaicans have loved Hominy Corn Porridge (page 75) for almost as long. Make sure you get the yellow hominy corn, not the white.

MOLASSES: A by-product of sugar production, molasses has a deep, rich flavor and is often added to sauces and baked goods. Jamaican Spice Bun (page 245) wouldn't be complete without a splash of molasses.

PEANUTS: Red-skinned peanuts are grown primarily on the south coast of Jamaica and are used in dishes like peanut porridge, Peanut Punch (page 295), and Peanut Drops (page 240). You can find them online and in many specialty stores, or you can use regular unsalted peanuts in a pinch.

RICE: Long-grain rice, particularly parboiled, is the most common rice in Jamaica, but jasmine rice is more fragrant and will make your Rice and Peas (page 127) taste even better. Make sure to rinse it three or four times to remove the excess starch and drain it in a sieve before cooking.

WATER CRACKERS: Originally designed for people who traveled long distances and needed food that would last, Excelsior Water Crackers are a favorite Jamaican snack. For more than one hundred years, this company has been using a unique wood-burning brick oven technique that makes its crackers somehow tough and fluffy at the same time. They are largely flavorless but are loved by Jamaicans from every corner of the island, eaten with Solomon Gundy (page 65), tinned mackerel, or tinned sardines or crumbled over porridge (page 73) for added texture.

JAMAICA

Yams
Falmouth
Montego Bay
Lucea
HANOVER
ST. JAMES
Turmeric
TRELAWNY
"The Breadbasket of Jamaica"
RUM
COCKPIT COUNTRY
WESTMORELAND
Sugarcane and ginger
Bammy
Savanna-la-Mar
Sugarcane
High-grade ganja
MANCHESTER
CLARENDON
ST. ELIZABETH
Mandeville
Appleton Estate
Black River
Pepper shrimp at Middlequarters
Sugarcane
Citrus and cassava
N
W
E
S
Rustic seafood at Little Ochi
CARIBBEAN SEA

CARIBBEAN SEA
Allspice
St. Ann's Bay
Bananas
Port Maria
ST. MARY
Blue Mountain Coffee
Cacao
ST. ANN
Boston Bay
Jerk Center
Port Antonio
ST. ANDREW
Beer
ST. CATHERINE
PORTLAND
Spanish Town
Kingston
May Pen
ST. THOMAS
Morant Bay
Fried fish and festival
at Hellshire Beach
Patties, ice cream at Devon House,
fresh produce at Coronation Market,
and cold Red Stripe Beer, made in
Kingston and available everywhere

WITH *Your* HANDS

BITE-SIZE TASTES OF JAMAICA

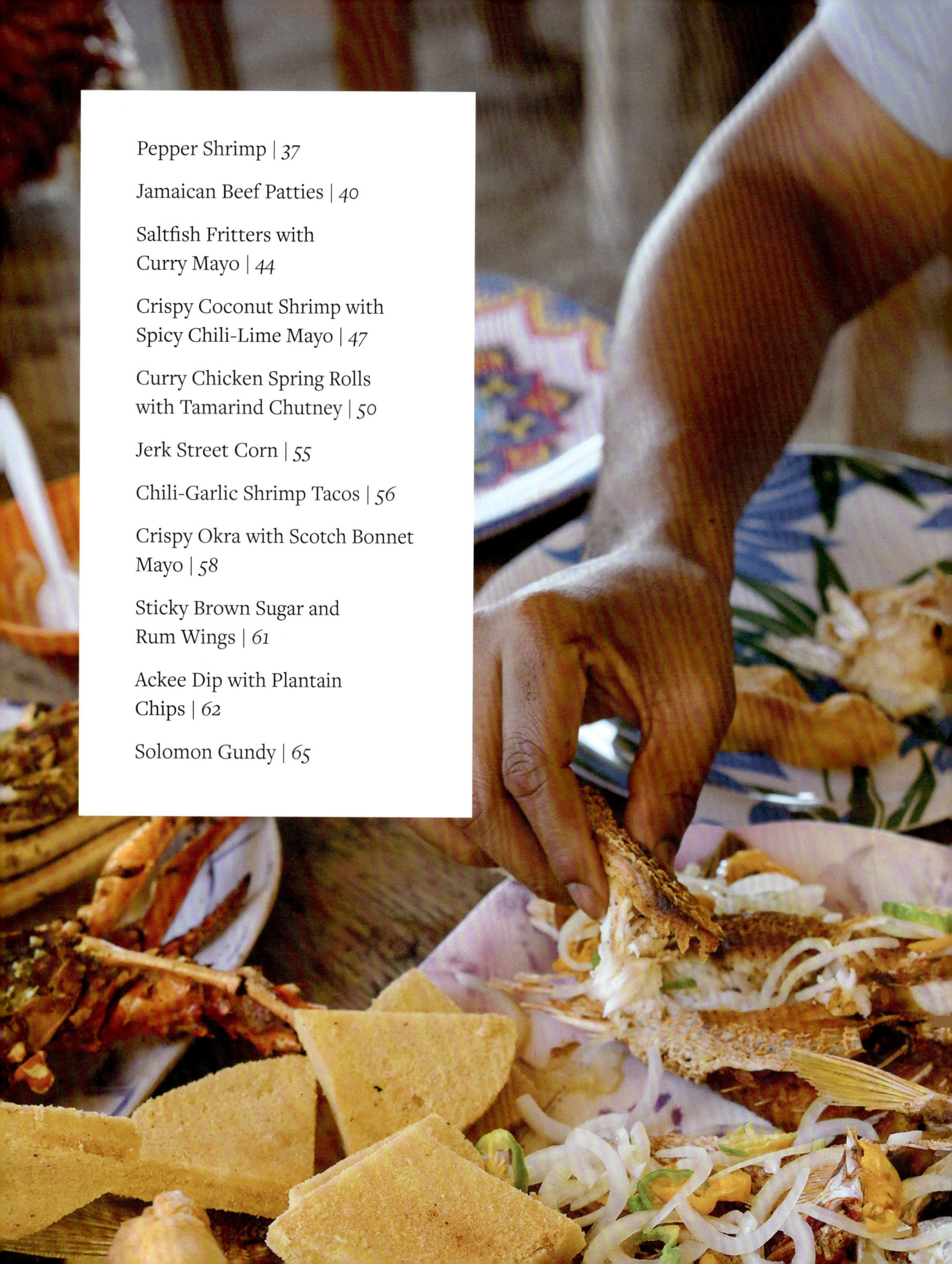

There's a simple joy in picking up a piece of food with your fingers and putting it in your mouth. Before it even gets to your tongue, you learn whether that food is soft or hard, rough or smooth, hot or cold. Your brain starts doing the math—will this be sweet, salty, bitter? And then you taste it. . . .

A lot of people would agree that food eaten with your hands actually tastes better. Think about the last time you ate fish and chips straight out of the wrapping paper, and the way the salt and vinegar clung to your fingers. Or that taco on the beach in Mexico, the salsa dripping out the end.

In Jamaica, the ultimate finger food is the Jamaican patty, whether it's filled with beef, curry chicken, or even vegetables. Patties have been a part of Jamaican culture since the seventeenth century, and their importance extends far beyond the island.

But patties are a labor of love, so if you're short on time and want a blast of flavor without all the effort, make Jerk Street Corn. With just a few basic ingredients and 30 minutes of prep time, you will have an irresistible snack with surprisingly complex flavors.

If you're craving salt, Solomon Gundy is the Jamaican cure. This traditional fish pâté is a bold, salty, and spicy spread, usually served with crackers or hard dough bread.

PEPPER SHRIMP

Serves 4 to 6

2 pounds (900 g) head-on large shrimp, deveined but with shells left on

4 garlic cloves, minced

4 scallions, thinly sliced

Leaves from 2 thyme sprigs

1 to 3 Scotch bonnet peppers (see Notes), minced

1 tablespoon vegetable oil or other neutral oil

1 tablespoon ground annatto (optional; see Notes)

1 tablespoon kosher salt, plus more to taste

2 teaspoons Old Bay seasoning (see Notes)

1 teaspoon freshly ground black pepper

¼ teaspoon ground allspice

½ cup (125 ml) distilled white vinegar

2 teaspoons sugar

No trip to "country"—which to a local means pretty much anywhere outside Kingston—is complete without stopping to buy pepper shrimp. *Peppa swims*, as they're known, are a fiery favorite roadside delicacy that first appeared in an area called Middle Quarters on Jamaica's south coast in the 1960s. There, they are small freshwater crayfish boiled in a briny, spicy broth loaded with Scotch bonnet peppers, allspice, and sometimes garlic and other spices. The result is a vibrant bright-red dish that packs a punch in both flavor and heat.

The simplicity of the preparation allows the natural sweetness of the shrimp to shine through the bold, aromatic spices. Though shrimp is in the recipe's name, the spicy bouillon is the star, and getting it right is like learning to fish—it will serve you well for a lifetime. Pile these on a platter with a bowl for shells (and lots of Wet-Naps on hand) and dig in.

Pat the shrimp dry with paper towels and place them in a large bowl. Add the garlic, scallions, thyme, Scotch bonnets, vegetable oil, annatto (if using), salt, Old Bay, black pepper, and allspice to the bowl and mix to coat the shrimp with the seasonings. Marinate in the fridge for 30 to 60 minutes.

Using gloves or a slotted spoon, transfer the shrimp to another bowl, leaving the vegetables and spices. Scrape the remaining marinade into a large saucepan and add 1 cup (250 ml) water. Bring to a simmer over medium heat, stirring occasionally, and cook until the sauce has reduced slightly and is fragrant, 8 to 10 minutes.

Add ¼ cup (60 ml) of the vinegar and the shrimp, cover the pan, increase the heat to high, and cook until the shrimp are opaque and fully cooked through, 4 to 7 minutes, stirring halfway through.

recipe continues

In a small bowl, stir together the remaining ¼ cup (60 ml) vinegar and the sugar, then pour the mixture over the shrimp and toss to coat fully. Season with more salt, if desired.

Transfer the shrimp to a serving plate and let cool slightly. Serve warm or at room temperature, along with bowls for the shells once they're peeled.

Store leftover shrimp with a little of the broth in an airtight container in the fridge for up to 3 days. You can serve leftover pepper shrimp cold or at room temperature.

NOTES

- Make sure to wear gloves while handling the peppers—they're hot!
- Swap the fresh Scotch bonnet peppers for 1 to 2 tablespoons Scotch Bonnet Sauce (page 310) or fresh habanero peppers. Adjust the spice levels to your taste.
- The ground annatto gives pepper shrimp their signature red color, but you can omit it if you can't find it.
- You can substitute your favorite all-purpose fish seasoning for the Old Bay.
- Save a little of the broth to keep leftovers in and toss the rest—it's too spicy to eat on its own.

PEPPER AND PLACE

Whenever I go to Jamaica these days, I stop at one of the colorful roadside shacks along the sprawling stretch of road through Middle Quarters on Jamaica's south coast. This is the original home of peppa swims, and though you can get versions of it elsewhere, Middle Quarters shrimp is the best. Most of what they sell here is actually freshwater crayfish—what we call janga in Jamaica. Shrimp are used instead when crayfish stocks run low, or by vendors in other parts of Jamaica.

Each vendor has a slightly different recipe, a family secret passed down through generations. But all their pepper shrimp have a rich, deep flavor and a distinctive shrimpy umami. The smaller shrimp are cooked enough that you can eat the whole thing from head to tail. The crunch adds yet another layer of complexity to these little delights.

You stand by the roadside, the sun beating down, with a cold Red Stripe in one hand and a bag bulging with pepper shrimp in the other. A vendor shouts, "Peppa swims! Peppa swims!" as a line of cars snake slowly past. The flavor hits you in waves—first the burn of the Scotch bonnet, then the rich depth of the allspice, and finally the sweetness of the shrimp itself. A sound system blares from the open windows of a country bus as it groans along the potholed road. Steam and smoke from the coal fire engulf your cook. This is the real Jamaica. This food is simple, unpretentious, and utterly satisfying.

JAMAICAN BEEF PATTIES

Makes 8 patties

For the patty dough

4 cups (500 g) all-purpose flour, plus more for rolling the dough

2 tablespoons sugar

1 tablespoon ground annatto

1 tablespoon kosher salt

2 teaspoons ground turmeric

¼ teaspoon baking powder

8 ounces (220 g) beef suet (see Notes), well chilled

1 cup (250 ml) ice water

1 tablespoon distilled white vinegar

1 egg

For the filling

1 tablespoon extra-virgin olive oil, vegetable oil, or other neutral oil

1 pound (450 g) ground beef, 80% lean

4 scallions, chopped

4 garlic cloves, minced

Leaves from 3 thyme sprigs

1 small yellow onion, chopped

½ Scotch bonnet pepper, seeded, or 1 to 2 teaspoons Scotch Bonnet Sauce (page 310)

1 tablespoon browning (see Notes)

2 teaspoons paprika

The Jamaican beef patty is the ultimate reflection of Jamaica's motto, "Out of Many, One People." Cornish sailors who arrived on the island to trade in sugar and spices in the seventeenth century brought with them the pasty, a flaky pastry filled with chunks of beef and vegetables. Indentured servants from India added to it their turmeric. Enslaved Africans brought the heat with bird peppers, and centuries later Chinese Jamaicans perfected mass production of the patty.

This delicious combination has made the patty Jamaica's most iconic street food. Though you can find great patties in Caribbean bakeries around the world, making your own gives you a deep appreciation for the technicality of this amazing handheld treat. The ingredients list is long, but the recipe is totally doable. Just take your time and follow the steps.

Make the patty dough: Sift the flour through a fine-mesh sieve into a large bowl. Add the sugar, annatto, salt, turmeric, and baking powder and mix to combine. Add the cold beef suet to the flour mixture and use your fingers or a fork to mix the fat into the dry ingredients until pea-sized bits of fat form.

In a separate bowl, whisk together the ice water, vinegar, and egg until well combined. Add the liquid to the dry ingredients and stir with a wooden spoon until a soft and shaggy dough forms.

In the same bowl, knead the dough with your hands until it's smooth, about 2 minutes. The dough should be soft enough that your finger leaves an imprint but not tacky or sticky. If it's too dry, add water, 1 tablespoon at a time, until it reaches the right consistency. Wrap the dough tightly in plastic wrap and let it rest in the fridge for at least 30 minutes.

Make the filling: Heat the oil in a large skillet over medium heat. Add the beef and stir to break it up. Cook until the meat starts to brown slightly, about 3 minutes.

1 teaspoon kosher salt, plus more to taste

1 teaspoon grated fresh ginger

1 teaspoon onion powder

1 teaspoon garlic powder

½ teaspoon ground allspice

½ teaspoon freshly ground black pepper

2 cups (500 ml) beef stock (see Notes)

2 slices white bread, or 1 cup (55 g) fresh bread crumbs

Coco bread, for serving (optional)

While the beef is cooking, in a food processor or blender, combine the scallions, garlic, thyme, onion, Scotch bonnet, browning, paprika, salt, ginger, onion powder, garlic powder, allspice, and black pepper. Process the mixture until a fine paste forms.

Transfer the seasoning blend to the skillet with the beef and stir to combine. Cook until the vegetables are fragrant, 2 to 3 minutes. Add the beef stock and stir, then cover the skillet, reduce the heat to medium-low, and cook, stirring occasionally, until the beef is tender, about 20 minutes. Meanwhile, in a blender, combine the slices of bread or bread crumbs with ½ cup (125 ml) water and blend until a thick paste forms. Add the paste to the skillet, stir, and cook for an additional 5 minutes, until the mixture is thick and velvety.

Assemble the patties: While the filling is cooling, line a sheet pan with parchment paper and dust a work surface with a generous sprinkle of flour. Roll the dough with a rolling pin until it is about ¼ inch (6 mm) thick, then fold the dough over itself twice. Repeat this process three more times, then shape the dough into a ball. Divide the ball of dough into 8 equal portions (see Notes), then roll each piece into a round about 8 inches (20 cm) in diameter and about ⅛ inch (3 mm) thick.

Divide the filling evenly among the dough rounds, placing it in the center of each one. Fold each round of dough over the filling into a half-moon shape, then seal the edges with a pastry wheel or fork. Place the patties on the lined sheet pan and put them in the fridge for at least 30 minutes to firm up.

When you're ready to bake, preheat the oven to 375°F (190°C). Bake the patties until golden brown and flaky, 25 to 30 minutes, rotating the pan front to back halfway through. For a true Jamaican experience, tuck your patty inside a sliced-open coco bread before eating.

NOTES

- Ask a butcher for ground beef suet or substitute 8 ounces (225 g) cold butter or vegetable shortening in a pinch, or if you'd prefer to make a vegetarian patty dough. Note that the texture won't be the same as with the suet.
- You can use bouillon paste or cubes dissolved in water in place of beef stock.
- Browning can be found in the international aisle of many grocery stores or at any Caribbean grocer.

recipe continues

- You can assemble the patties ahead of time and freeze them on the sheet pan until solid. Transfer the frozen patties to a ziplock bag and freeze for up to 3 months. Bake them directly from the freezer, adding an extra 5 minutes to the cooking time.
- To make mini patties, divide the dough into 12 pieces and follow the recipe.

VARIATIONS

Want to try a different patty? Swap the beef filling for Ackee and Saltfish (page 78), Steamed Callaloo (page 81), Curry Goat (page 170, meat picked off the bone), Coconut Curry Lobster (page 171, meat picked from the shell and chopped), or Almost Ital Curry Vegetable Stew (page 175).

PATTY WARS

The Jamaican beef patty sparked a food fight in Canada in the 1980s. First introduced to the country by West Indian immigrants during the 1960s and '70s, the beef patty, as it was known all over the Caribbean, quickly became a sought-after snack in Toronto. In 1985, the "Patty Wars" erupted when the Canadian government tried to legislate the name "beef patty," arguing that it conflicted with their definition of a beef patty as containing only meat and seasoning and not encased in dough or a crust. Michael Davidson, manager of Kensington Patty Palace, and other Jamaican bakery owners stood up to defend their cultural staple.

Despite the threat of steep fines, patty vendors banded together and refused to sell the iconic pastry under any other name. Politicians, lawyers, and even the Jamaican consulate got involved. Caribbean people around the country claimed their heritage was being destroyed. The government made suggestions for a new name: Turnover. Caribbean Meat Pocket. Handheld Pocket. Caribbean Pie. The response from Davidson and his lawyer was a firm no. He explained the patty's deep cultural importance and likened the name change to renaming poutine "fries with sauce and cheese bits" or donuts "sugar circles."

As a compromise, the vendors agreed not to use the term "beef patty," but they could call their product a "Jamaican patty." This victory is celebrated every February 23 as Patty Day in Toronto, a delicious reminder of the passion of Jamaican Canadians.

SALTFISH FRITTERS *with* CURRY MAYO

Serves 8

For the curry mayo

2 tablespoons extra-virgin olive oil

1 shallot, finely diced

1 garlic clove, minced

1 teaspoon grated fresh ginger

1 tablespoon Jamaican curry powder

1 cup (225 g) mayonnaise

Grated zest and juice of 1 lime

Kosher salt and freshly ground black pepper

For the saltfish fritters

8 ounces (225 g) boneless salt cod, prepared (see page 46) and shredded

½ medium onion, finely diced

½ red bell pepper, finely diced

½ Scotch bonnet pepper, seeded and minced

Leaves from 2 thyme sprigs

2 scallions, minced

1 garlic clove, minced

1 cup (125 g) all-purpose flour

2 teaspoons baking powder

1 teaspoon garlic powder

1 teaspoon onion powder

Saltfish fritters—also known as Stamp and Go—are Jamaica's original fast food. Their intense flavor comes from the batter mix: flaked saltfish, fresh herbs and spices, and, of course, Scotch bonnet pepper. This version is a riff on traditional fritters, which are flat and denser. The addition of baking powder makes these puffy delights one of the most addictive things you'll ever eat: crispy on the outside, soft and spicy on the inside. Served with a curry mayo for dipping, these are perfect for a party platter or just when you feel like having a delicious snack.

Make the curry mayo: Heat the oil in a small skillet over medium-low heat. Add the shallot and cook until soft, 2 to 3 minutes. Add the garlic and ginger and cook until fragrant, another minute or so. Add the curry powder and cook, stirring constantly, until fragrant, about 1 minute.

Transfer the curry and shallot mixture to a small bowl and add the mayonnaise and lime zest and juice. Season to taste with salt and pepper. (Curry mayo can be stored in an airtight container in the fridge for up to 1 week.)

Make the saltfish fritters: In a medium bowl, combine the shredded cod, onion, bell pepper, Scotch bonnet, thyme, scallions, and garlic. Stir with a silicone spatula to combine, then add the flour, baking powder, garlic powder, onion powder, allspice, salt, and pepper. Mix again to coat the fish and vegetables thoroughly in the flour and spices. Add the egg and milk to the bowl and stir until just combined. The batter should be as thick as pancake batter.

Line a plate with paper towels and set it near the stove. Pour about 3 inches (7.5 cm) of oil into a medium saucepan and heat over medium-high heat to 350°F (177°C), or until the oil sizzles around a wooden spoon when it's dipped in the hot oil.

½ teaspoon ground allspice

½ teaspoon kosher salt

½ teaspoon freshly ground black pepper

1 egg, lightly beaten

½ cup (125 ml) milk or water

Vegetable oil or other neutral oil, for deep-frying

Working in batches, use a 1-ounce (30 ml) scoop or a heaping tablespoon to drop scoops of the batter into the hot oil. Fry until the fritters are golden brown and fully cooked inside, 3 to 4 minutes, flipping halfway through if they don't flip on their own. With a slotted spoon, transfer the cooked fritters to the paper towels to drain. Continue cooking until all the batter has been used up.

Serve hot with the curry mayo.

HOW TO PREPARE SALT COD (SALTFISH)

Not all saltfish is created equal. Boneless, skinless saltfish costs more, but is easier to work with. Look for fillets that are firm and have a consistent white to off-white color, and avoid pieces with dark spots or yellowing. Products stored in airtight, well-sealed bags will maintain quality. Out of the package, salt cod should have a clean, salty aroma, not too fishy or unpleasant. The intense saltiness and tough texture make salt cod unpalatable until it's been soaked and cooked to mellow the flavor and tenderize the meat. There are two ways to prepare saltfish: soaking or boiling. I prefer the soaking method, but if you're short on time, the boiling method will do just fine. If the cod fillet is large, cut it into smaller pieces.

THE SOAKING METHOD

Soaking removes excess salt from the fish and rehydrates the flesh, resulting in a moist and delicate texture.

1. Rinse the saltfish under cold water to remove excess salt.
2. Fully submerge the saltfish in a bowl of cold water and soak for 6 to 12 hours in the fridge, changing the water at least once during this time.
3. Discard the soaking water. Taste a small piece of the saltfish.
4. If the fish is still too salty, place it in a pot and cover with fresh water. Bring to a boil over medium heat and cook for 5 to 10 minutes, until the flesh is plump and tender. Then transfer the fish to a plate and let cool.
5. Use your fingers to break the saltfish into smaller flakes.

THE BOILING METHOD

This method quickly reduces saltiness, but the result isn't as delicate.

1. Rinse the saltfish under cold water to remove excess salt.
2. Place the saltfish in a pot and cover with fresh water. Bring to a boil over medium heat, then reduce the heat and simmer for 10 to 20 minutes, depending on the thickness of the cod.
3. Discard the boiling water and repeat the process if necessary to reduce the saltiness. Once the fish tastes well-seasoned (but not overly salty), it's ready to be used.
4. Transfer the cod to a plate and let cool, then use your fingers to break the saltfish into smaller flakes.

CRISPY COCONUT SHRIMP *with* SPICY CHILI-LIME MAYO

Serves 4

For the chili-lime mayo

½ cup (110 g) mayonnaise

2 tablespoons sriracha

1 tablespoon chili-garlic paste (see Note)

1 teaspoon soy sauce

1 garlic clove, minced

Grated zest and juice of 1 lime

For the coconut shrimp

1 pound (450 g) large shrimp, peeled and deveined

1 tablespoon extra-virgin olive oil

2 teaspoons kosher salt

1 teaspoon freshly ground black pepper

½ teaspoon garlic powder

½ teaspoon onion powder

1 cup (125 g) all-purpose flour

2 large eggs

2 cups (170 g) sweetened coconut flakes

½ cup (50 g) panko bread crumbs

Vegetable oil or other neutral oil, for deep-frying

Chopped fresh cilantro, for serving (optional)

Lime wedges, for serving (optional)

These deep-fried coconut shrimp are a perfect blend of crunchy, tender, sweet, and spicy. The texture of the shrimp is maintained by the golden layer of crispy coconut, but make sure you don't overcook them (the tail will be slightly curled when fully cooked). The spicy chili-lime mayo and a squeeze of fresh lime juice are the icing on this cake. These bingeable coconut shrimp are easy to make and perfect for any occasion. Plus, they'll make you look like a great cook!

Make the chili-lime mayo: In a small bowl, stir together the mayonnaise, sriracha, chili-garlic paste, soy sauce, garlic, lime zest, and lime juice. Set aside.

Make the coconut shrimp: In a medium bowl, stir together the shrimp, olive oil, 1 teaspoon of the salt, ½ teaspoon of the pepper, the garlic powder, and the onion powder.

Set up a dredging station in three shallow bowls: In the first bowl, combine the flour, the remaining 1 teaspoon salt, and the remaining ½ teaspoon pepper. Add the eggs and a splash of water to the second bowl and mix well with a fork. Combine the coconut flakes and panko in the third bowl.

Line a plate with paper towels and set it near the stove. Pour about 2 inches (5 cm) of oil into a large saucepan and heat over medium heat to 350°F (177°C), or until the oil sizzles around a wooden spoon when it's dipped in the hot oil.

While the oil is heating, bread the shrimp, working in batches, by coating them in the flour and shaking off any excess. Transfer the shrimp to the egg mixture and toss to coat fully. Finally, dip the shrimp into the coconut-panko mix, pressing some of the mixture into the shrimp to make sure it sticks.

recipe continues

Working in batches, fry the shrimp until golden brown and fully cooked, 1 to 2 minutes on each side. With a slotted spoon, transfer them to the paper towels to drain.

Serve immediately with chopped cilantro (if desired), lime wedges (if desired), and the chili-lime mayo for dipping.

NOTE: Chili-garlic paste intensifies the flavor in this dish—you can usually find it in the Asian section of the grocery store. If you can't find any, add more sriracha instead (you won't get the same depth of flavor without it, though!).

CURRY CHICKEN SPRING ROLLS *with* TAMARIND CHUTNEY

Serves 6

1 tablespoon all-purpose flour or cornstarch

One 12-ounce (340 g) package spring roll or egg roll wrappers

2 cups (250 g) leftover Curry Chicken (page 169), shredded

Vegetable oil or other neutral oil, for deep-frying

Tamarind Chutney (recipe follows)

This is a creative twist on spring rolls that combines Jamaica's Indian, African, and Chinese flavors. And these rolls are the best imaginable way to use leftover curry chicken. Tamarind is an evergreen tree related to peas, and the fruit grows in pods just like the peas in your garden. Inside the pod are large seeds surrounded by a sticky, dark brown pulp. This pulp is what's used in cooking. It brings a unique blend of sour and sweet and plays a crucial role in balancing flavors in spicy, more complex dishes.

In a small bowl, combine the flour and 2 tablespoons water and set near your work station. Peel off one spring roll wrapper and cover the rest with a damp paper towel or plastic wrap so they don't dry out. Lay the spring roll wrapper on a plate or cutting board in a diamond orientation, then spoon 1 to 2 tablespoons of shredded curry chicken onto the bottom of the wrapper. Roll it up halfway, then fold the sides in. Brush a small amount of the flour paste onto the end of the wrapper with your finger or a pastry brush, then finish rolling the spring roll to seal the end. Repeat until you've used up all the filling.

Line a plate with paper towels and set it near the stove. Pour about 2 inches (5 cm) of vegetable oil into a medium saucepan and heat over medium-high heat to 350°F (177°C), or until the oil sizzles around a wooden spoon when it's dipped in the hot oil.

Working in batches to avoid overcrowding, carefully place the spring rolls in the oil and fry until golden brown, 3 to 5 minutes. Using a slotted spoon, transfer the cooked spring rolls to the paper towels to drain.

Serve immediately with tamarind chutney.

recipe continues

NOTE: You can assemble these spring rolls ahead of time. Once you've stuffed and rolled the spring rolls, lay them on a baking sheet lined with parchment paper and freeze them. After they're frozen, you can transfer the spring rolls to a freezer storage bag or container. Fry them from frozen when you're ready to cook them, but make sure to heat them all the way through (7 to 9 minutes).

VARIATION

Vegetarian Spring Rolls: Use Almost Ital Curry Vegetable Stew (page 175) instead of the curry chicken for the filling.

Tamarind Chutney

Makes just over 1 cup (300 to 325 ml)

½ cup (110 g) packed light brown sugar

2 tablespoons tamarind paste or concentrate

1 tablespoon grated fresh ginger

1 teaspoon ground cumin

1 teaspoon kosher salt

½ teaspoon chili powder

½ teaspoon smoked paprika

½ teaspoon garlic powder

4 dates, pitted

In a small saucepan, combine 1 cup (250 ml) water with the brown sugar, tamarind paste, ginger, cumin, salt, chili powder, smoked paprika, garlic powder, and dates. Bring to a simmer over medium heat and cook until the dates have softened and the sauce has reduced slightly, 8 to 10 minutes.

Transfer to a blender and blend until smooth. Store in an airtight container in the fridge for up to 2 weeks.

JERK STREET CORN

Serves 4 to 6

4 ears corn, shucked and cut in half

One 14-ounce (400 ml) can coconut milk (1¾ cups)

¼ cup (50 g) sugar

1 tablespoon kosher salt

2 cinnamon sticks

Eight 6-inch (15 cm) wooden skewers

½ cup (110 g) Jerk Mayo (page 319)

1 cup (85 g) sweetened shredded coconut, lightly toasted (see Note)

1 lime, for serving

Corn on the cob boiled in a spicy broth is a popular Jamaican street food. We don't fuss with it—we just eat it piping hot with chunks of coconut served on the side. This is an upscale reimagining of that simple snack, and it's always a hit.

Grilling the corn after it's cooked intensifies the flavors, but by far the most important ingredient is the lime—it ties everything together for a perfect bite.

In a large saucepan, combine the corn, coconut milk, sugar, salt, and cinnamon sticks, with enough water to just cover the corn. Bring to a boil over high heat, then reduce the heat to medium-low and simmer until the corn is soft and flavorful, about 15 minutes.

Drain the corn in a colander over the sink and let it sit for 5 minutes to allow any excess liquid to drain.

For extra flavor, cook the corn on a grill preheated to 425°F (220°C) until char marks develop on all sides of the corn, 3 to 5 minutes, turning frequently. Alternatively, you can sear the corn in a grill pan on the stove over high heat. If you don't have a grill or a grill pan, you can skip this step. Just make sure to pat the corn dry with paper towels before the next step.

Once the corn is cool enough to handle, put a skewer through each piece and brush them evenly with the jerk mayo using a pastry brush. Spread the toasted coconut on a plate and roll the corn in the coconut. You may need to use your hands to press some of the toasted coconut into the corn to ensure it is coated evenly.

Arrange the corn on a platter. Using a zester or fine grater, zest the lime over the top of the corn. Cut the lime into wedges. Serve the corn immediately with the lime wedges.

NOTE: To toast the shredded coconut, preheat the oven to 325°F (160°C) and line a baking sheet with parchment paper. Spread the coconut on the pan in an even layer and bake until golden brown, 4 to 6 minutes, stirring halfway through.

CHILI-GARLIC SHRIMP TACOS

Makes 8 tacos

For the Scotch bonnet–cilantro sauce

½ cup (125 g) sour cream or whole-milk Greek yogurt

1 tablespoon extra-virgin olive oil

1 teaspoon kosher salt

1 teaspoon Scotch Bonnet Sauce (page 310)

2 scallions, minced

2 garlic cloves, minced

Handful of fresh cilantro, chopped

Grated zest and juice of 1 lime

For the shrimp tacos

1 pound (450 g) large shrimp, peeled and deveined

3 tablespoons extra-virgin olive oil

1 tablespoon chili-garlic paste

1 teaspoon kosher salt, plus more to taste

½ teaspoon garlic powder

½ teaspoon onion powder

½ teaspoon smoked paprika

¼ teaspoon chile flakes

¼ teaspoon freshly ground black pepper, plus more to taste

These shrimp tacos come alive with the bold, spicy kick of the Scotch bonnet–cilantro sauce. The creamy dressing is easy to whip up and adds a zesty, herbaceous flavor that perfectly balances the heat. Paired with tender shrimp and crisp cabbage, the sauce transforms a simple taco into a vibrant, satisfying meal. If you can't find large shrimp, use smaller ones but make sure to reduce the time they spend in the pan.

Make the Scotch bonnet–cilantro sauce: In a small bowl, combine the sour cream, olive oil, salt, Scotch bonnet sauce, scallions, garlic, cilantro, lime zest, and lime juice. Whisk to combine and set aside until needed. (The sauce can be made up to 3 days ahead and stored in an airtight container in the fridge.)

Make the shrimp tacos: Pat the shrimp dry with paper towels. In a medium bowl, combine the shrimp, 1 tablespoon of the olive oil, chili-garlic paste, salt, garlic powder, onion powder, smoked paprika, chile flakes, and black pepper. Toss to coat the shrimp fully in the spices. Set aside.

In a separate large bowl, combine the shredded cabbage and half the Scotch bonnet–cilantro sauce and stir to combine. Season to taste with salt and pepper, if necessary. Set aside.

Heat a large skillet over medium-high heat. Depending on the size of your pan, heat 1 to 3 tortillas at a time until lightly browned on both sides, 30 to 60 seconds per side. Repeat until all the tortillas are warmed. Wrap the warmed tortillas in aluminum foil or a clean tea towel and set aside until ready to serve.

Heat the remaining 2 tablespoons olive oil in the same skillet over medium-high heat. Add the shrimp to the hot pan and sear until fully cooked and no longer translucent, 4 to 6 minutes, flipping halfway through.

¼ small head green cabbage, thinly sliced

8 small flour or corn tortillas

2 small avocados, smashed

½ batch Pickled Red Onions (page 158)

1 jalapeño pepper (optional), thinly sliced

Handful of fresh cilantro, leaves torn

1 lime, cut into wedges

To assemble the tacos, top each tortilla with some smashed avocado, shredded cabbage, shrimp, pickled red onion, sliced jalapeño (if using), torn cilantro, and remaining Scotch bonnet–cilantro sauce. Serve immediately with lime wedges. Store leftover components (not assembled tacos) in airtight containers in the fridge for up to 2 days.

CRISPY OKRA *with* SCOTCH BONNET MAYO

Serves 6

- Vegetable oil or other neutral oil, for deep-frying
- 1 pound (450 g) fresh okra, stems trimmed
- ½ cup (60 g) plus 2 tablespoons all-purpose flour
- ½ cup (60 g) cornstarch
- 1 tablespoon kosher salt, plus more to taste
- 1 teaspoon onion powder
- 1 teaspoon garlic powder
- ½ teaspoon smoked paprika
- ½ teaspoon freshly ground black pepper
- 1 to 1½ cups (250 to 375 ml) cold club soda
- Scotch Bonnet Mayo (page 319), for serving

Even sworn okra haters will swoon at these crunchy okra fingers. This recipe delivers perfectly crispy bites without any of the sliminess we usually associate with okra. The secret lies in getting them into the hot oil as soon as possible after cutting and battering them. The result is a crunchy exterior that locks in the tender interior, all without the unwanted texture. Paired with a spicy Scotch bonnet mayo for dipping, these fried okra pieces are an irresistible snack or side dish.

Line a plate with paper towels and set it near the stove. Pour 2 to 3 inches (5 to 7.5 cm) of oil into a large saucepan and heat over medium-high heat to 350°F (177°C), or until the oil sizzles around a wooden spoon when it's dipped in the hot oil.

While the oil is heating, slice the okra pods in half lengthwise and sprinkle them with 2 tablespoons flour. Toss to coat and set aside.

In a medium bowl, whisk together the remaining ½ cup (60 g) flour with the cornstarch, salt, onion powder, garlic powder, smoked paprika, and black pepper. Add 1 cup (250 ml) of the club soda to the dry ingredients and whisk until just combined. The batter should be as runny as crepe batter. If it's too thick, whisk in the remaining ½ cup (125 ml) club soda.

Working in batches so you don't overcrowd the pan, dip each okra piece into the batter and swirl it around briefly to fully coat. Let the excess batter drip off, then carefully place the battered okra in the hot oil. Fry until golden brown and crispy, 3 to 4 minutes. Transfer the fried okra to the paper towels to drain. Continue until all the okra pieces have been fried. Sprinkle a little salt on the okra before serving, if desired.

Serve immediately with Scotch bonnet mayo.

STICKY BROWN SUGAR AND RUM WINGS

Serves 4

For the glaze

½ cup (110 g) packed light brown sugar

2 tablespoons dark rum

2 tablespoons sriracha

2 tablespoons reduced-sodium soy sauce

1 teaspoon Scotch Bonnet Sauce (page 310)

2 garlic cloves, minced

3 tablespoons (1.5 ounces/45 g) cold unsalted butter, cut into small pieces

For the wings

3 pounds (1.4 kg) chicken wings (no tips), split at the joint into flats and drumettes

3 tablespoons vegetable oil or other neutral oil

2 tablespoons Dry Jerk Rub (page 317) or store-bought jerk seasoning

1 tablespoon kosher salt

1 teaspoon garlic powder

1 teaspoon onion powder

1 teaspoon smoked paprika

½ teaspoon freshly ground black pepper

Jamaica is renowned for its rum, adhering to strict standards that produce some of the world's finest. Rum is more than just a drink here; it's a key part of the culture, adding depth and warmth to both celebrations and the kitchen. And here it is, making magic in a rich, sweet, and spicy glaze. The glaze comes together in minutes, adding a sticky, flavorful finish that perfectly complements the jerk-spiced wings. With minimal prep and an easy baking method, these are sure to impress. Serve them for dinner or at a party, and make sure you eat them with your hands.

Make the glaze: In a small saucepan, whisk together the brown sugar, rum, sriracha, soy sauce, Scotch bonnet sauce, and garlic. Bring to a boil over high heat, then reduce the heat to medium-low and cook, stirring frequently, until syrupy, 4 to 6 minutes. Remove from the heat and whisk in the butter. Set aside.

Cook the wings: Preheat the oven to 425°F (220°C). Line a sheet pan with aluminum foil and place a wire rack on top of the foil.

Pat the chicken wings dry with paper towels and put them in a large bowl along with the oil, dry jerk rub, salt, garlic powder, onion powder, smoked paprika, and black pepper. Toss to coat the wings in the spices.

Line the wings on the wire rack, making sure not to overcrowd the pan. Bake until the wings are fully cooked, about 45 minutes, flipping halfway through.

Transfer the wings to a clean bowl and pour the glaze over them. Toss the wings to coat them fully and serve immediately. Store leftovers in an airtight container in the fridge for up to 4 days. Reheat in a 350°F (180°C) oven for 10 to 12 minutes.

ACKEE DIP *with* PLANTAIN CHIPS

Serves 4

For the plantain chips

Vegetable oil or other neutral oil, for deep-frying

2 green plantains (see Note), peeled

Kosher salt

For the ackee dip

One 19-ounce (540 g) can ackee, drained and rinsed

3 garlic cloves, minced

Leaves from 2 thyme sprigs, chopped

1 scallion, minced

1 small shallot, minced

Grated zest and juice of 1 lime

1 jalapeño pepper, seeded and minced

2 tablespoons extra-virgin olive oil

1 teaspoon kosher salt

½ teaspoon smoked paprika

½ teaspoon garlic powder

½ teaspoon onion powder

½ teaspoon freshly ground black pepper

Handful of fresh cilantro, chopped

The buttery goodness of ackee makes it perfect for dip-making. Enhanced with garlic, thyme, a little heat, and some essential seasoning, this deeply savory spread is my rendition of hummus but lighter and more delicate. The homemade plantain chips have a satisfying crunch and are sturdy enough to scoop the dip. Serve this as part of a grazing table, as passed hors d'oeuvres, or for snacking during family board game night.

Make the plantain chips: Pour 2 inches (5 cm) of oil into a wide saucepan and heat over medium heat to 325°F (163°C). Line a plate with paper towels and set it near the stove.

Slice plantains ⅛ inch (3 mm) thick (or thinner if you prefer a lighter chip) using a mandoline, vegetable peeler, or sharp knife. You can slice the plantains into round coins or long, thin strips. Add the plantain slices to the hot oil and fry until golden brown and crispy, 3 to 5 minutes. Transfer the plantain chips to the paper towels and season generously with salt. (Plantain chips will keep in an airtight container at room temperature for up to 1 week.)

Make the ackee dip: In a food processor, combine the ackee, garlic, thyme, scallion, shallot, lime zest, lime juice, jalapeño, olive oil, salt, smoked paprika, garlic powder, onion powder, black pepper, and cilantro and blend to combine. Taste for seasoning and adjust as necessary. Transfer to a bowl or airtight container, cover, and refrigerate for at least 30 minutes to let the flavors come together.

Serve chilled or at room temperature with plantain chips. Store leftover dip in an airtight container in the fridge for up to 3 days.

NOTE: The greener the plantain, the crispier your chips will be. Riper plantain tends to get soggy quickly and burns easily while frying.

ACKEE: A DELICIOUS ENIGMA

Ackee, Jamaica's national fruit, is as mouthwatering as it is mysterious. Twice a year, clusters of swollen pods in shades of gold and red hang heavy under the glossy green canopy of the ackee tree. The fruits are beautiful and delicious, but they hold a dark secret: Unripe ackee flesh, the seeds, and the pinkish membrane at the base of the seeds contain large quantities of two toxic molecules, hypoglycin A and hypoglycin B. If the fruit hasn't ripened enough to burst open on its own, revealing glossy black seeds and yellow flesh, eating it can make you very sick or even kill you. *Time* magazine once ranked ackee among the world's top ten most dangerous foods. The FDA banned the import of ackee to the United States in 1973. And long before that—around 1900—ackee was banned in Trinidad after several ackee-related fatalities.

And yet in 2012, the NatGeo World Food Tour named ackee and saltfish the second-best national dish in the world. Fresh, ripe ackee is sold all over Jamaica—at roadside stands, at markets, and in the supermarket too—and of course is half the duo in our national dish (see the recipe on page 78).

A lengthy lobbying campaign by the Jamaica Ackee Task Force led to the U.S. ban being partially lifted in 2000, and since then, under strict regulations, canned and frozen ackee are allowed into the United States.

Ackee's reputation may have limited its popularity abroad, but its story adds an intriguing twist to this alluring Jamaican fruit.

SOLOMON GUNDY

Serves 6

1 pound (450 g) salted smoked herring fillets (see Note)

5 garlic cloves, smashed and peeled

Leaves from 3 thyme sprigs

2 scallions, chopped

2 Scotch bonnet or habanero peppers, chopped

1 shallot or ½ small red onion, chopped

½ cup (125 ml) distilled white vinegar

¼ cup (60 ml) vegetable oil or other neutral oil

1 tablespoon molasses

2 teaspoons paprika

2 teaspoons onion powder

2 teaspoons garlic powder

1 teaspoon kosher salt

½ teaspoon allspice berries

¼ teaspoon freshly grated nutmeg

Crackers, for serving

The name for this dish is hard to pin down—maybe it's from an obscure French word roughly meaning hodgepodge or from an Italian phrase for pickled meat. Wherever it's from, the essential root word is *sal*, meaning salt or seasoning. Jamaican Solomon Gundy is a pâté made of smoked salted herring, seasonings, and just enough Scotch bonnet heat. This spread is traditionally served on water crackers as a savory snack, but it makes a unique canapé on top of Pressed Green Plantain (page 133) with a tiny dollop of Jerk Mayo (page 319).

Place the herring in a large heatproof bowl and add enough boiling water to cover the fish. Soak the fish in the hot water for 10 minutes to get rid of excess salt. Drain the fish, then use your hands to shred the herring, removing as many of the fine bones as you can.

In a food processor or blender, combine the garlic, thyme, scallions, Scotch bonnets, shallot, vinegar, oil, molasses, paprika, onion powder, garlic powder, salt, allspice berries, and nutmeg and pulse to form a paste. Add the shredded herring and pulse once more to combine.

Serve with crackers. Store in an airtight container in the fridge for up to 2 weeks. This dish gets better as it ages.

NOTE: This recipe calls for salted smoked herring fillets, not the canned variety. Smoked herring can be found near the meat and seafood section of many supermarkets (especially Latin American and Caribbean stores).

recipe continues

Clockwise from top: Solomon Gundy, Ackee Dip (page 62), Solomon Gundy Dip (page 66), Plantain Chips (page 62).

VARIATION

Solomon Gundy Dip: For a delicious dip, mix some prepared Solomon Gundy with cream cheese, starting with a 1:2 ratio of Solomon Gundy to cream cheese. Add more or less cream cheese to taste. You can add sour cream, fresh thyme leaves, extra garlic, chopped shallots, and/or lime juice to boost the flavor. Season to taste with kosher salt and freshly ground black pepper and serve with your favorite crackers for a quick appetizer.

SOLOMON GUNDY AND THE BAY OF FUNDY

Solomon Gundy is said to have been popular with pirates and buccaneers in the seventeenth and eighteenth centuries. A British cookbook published in 1741 included a recipe for Solomon Gundy, with the instruction to "shred" the herring and other ingredients. It uses lime peel—no doubt from one of the colonies—to "pickle" the salted herring. These days, Solomon Gundy is almost impossible to find in contemporary English cuisine.

In the 1770s, George Washington's slaves caught about a million herring in the Potomac River each year. The fish were cleaned and packed into wooden barrels, separated by layers of salt, and shipped abroad. Much of it went to the Caribbean to feed enslaved people harvesting sugarcane, which then left the islands as rum and molasses.

In Nova Scotia on Canada's east coast, Solomon Gundy has been a traditional snack for generations, but nobody can say exactly where it came from. There, it's a simple pickled herring, usually served on a cracker with a generous layer of cream cheese. It's making a comeback now. Oh, and the herring for this Solomon Gundy? It comes from the Bay of Fundy.

91
ELLETH IN
PLACE
T HIGH
UNDER THE
F THE
ITY
THE LORD IS
STRENGHT OF MY LIFE
WHOM SHALL I
RED STRIPE
DRAGON
GUINNESS
BOX JUICE
SOLD HERE
MAGNUM
BIG JO BOX DRINK

RISE *and* SHINE

BREAKFAST

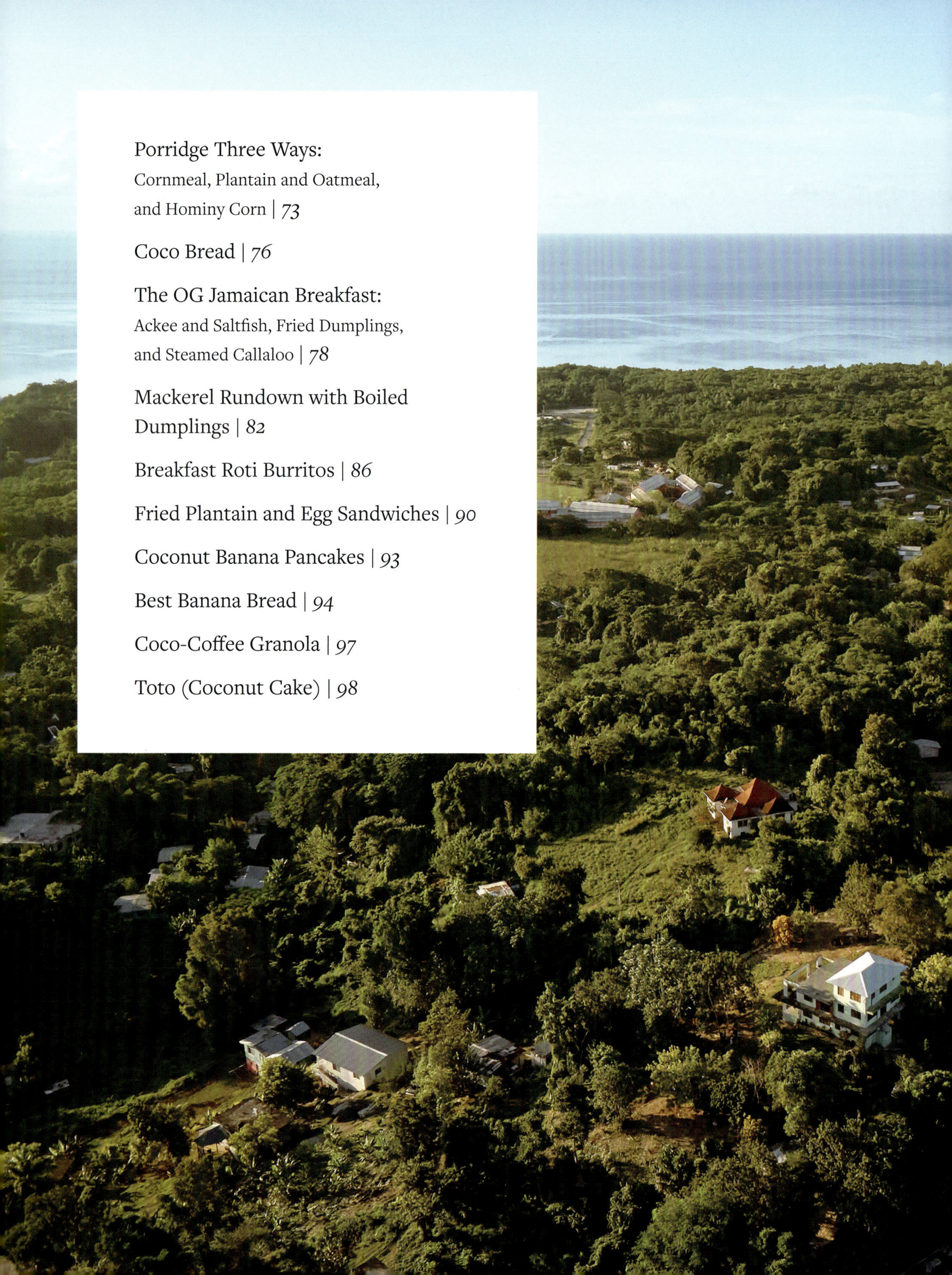

Reggae music blares from the neighbor's radio.

Sunlight and shadows dance in the palm fronds.

The ksh-ksh-ksh of a thatch broom scratches concrete.

Now add the smell of dumplings in hot oil and your Jamaican morning is nearly complete.

Whether it's the start of a workday or a lazy Sunday, a traditional island breakfast will make you rise and shine to meet whatever life throws at you. Make the Cornmeal Porridge for an easy weekday breakfast, or try the Best Banana Bread to bring to brunch at a friend's house. If you're feeling adventurous and you're ready for a full-immersion experience in Jamaican cooking, make the OG Jamaican Breakfast for a weekend feast. These breakfast recipes are not just local favorites (and my twists on a few); some of them are the first dishes I learned from my mother, Patsy, and my grandmother Mama Cherry.

PORRIDGE THREE WAYS

CORNMEAL, PLANTAIN AND OATMEAL, AND HOMINY CORN

When a Jamaican says *porridge*, we don't mean just oatmeal. We have different kinds of porridge: cornmeal, plantain, hominy, peanut, green banana, and bulgur, to name a few. And even our oats porridge (as we call oatmeal) is elevated with warming spices like nutmeg, cinnamon, and allspice. The recipes that follow are my family's favorites. In all of them, you can swap the condensed milk for honey, brown sugar, or your sweetener of choice. You can also reduce the amount of sweetener to suit your taste. I love mine super sweet, topped with crushed water crackers and an extra drizzle of condensed milk.

CORNMEAL PORRIDGE

Serves 4 to 6

One 14-ounce (400 ml) can coconut milk (1¾ cups)

1 strip of orange zest, 2 to 3 inches (5 to 7.5 cm) long

2 cinnamon sticks or ½ teaspoon ground cinnamon

6 allspice berries or ¼ teaspoon ground allspice

1 cup (160 g) fine yellow cornmeal

1 cup (250 ml) sweetened condensed milk

2 teaspoons pure vanilla extract

½ teaspoon freshly grated nutmeg

½ teaspoon kosher salt

In a medium saucepan, combine 2 cups (500 ml) water with the coconut milk, orange zest, cinnamon, and allspice berries and bring to a boil over high heat. Reduce the heat to medium and cook for 2 minutes.

In a small bowl, whisk together 2 cups (500 ml) water and the cornmeal to create a slurry. Slowly pour the cornmeal mixture into the saucepan with the hot liquid while whisking vigorously. Reduce the heat to low and simmer until the cornmeal grains are soft, about 15 minutes.

Add the condensed milk, vanilla, nutmeg, and salt. Stir to combine.

Remove from the heat, discard the orange zest strip, cinnamon sticks, and allspice berries (if used), and serve immediately.

Store leftovers in an airtight container in the fridge for up to 2 days. Reheat in the microwave or in a small saucepan over low heat. You may need to add a splash of water to help loosen the porridge.

recipes continue

PLANTAIN AND OATMEAL PORRIDGE

Serves 6

1 large green plantain, peeled and cut into 1-inch (2.5 cm) pieces

1 cup (90 g) quick-cooking oats

One 14-ounce (400 ml) can coconut milk (1¾ cups)

1 cup (250 ml) sweetened condensed milk, plus more to taste

1 tablespoon pure vanilla extract

½ teaspoon ground cinnamon

½ teaspoon freshly grated nutmeg

½ teaspoon kosher salt

Bring 3 cups (750 ml) water to a boil in a large saucepan over high heat.

While the water is coming to a boil, in a blender, combine 3 cups (750 ml) water, the green plantain, and the oats and blend until smooth.

Pour the blended plantain and oat mixture into the pot of boiling water while whisking vigorously. Once combined, cover, reduce the heat to medium, and cook until thick and creamy, about 20 minutes. It will be a very thick mixture, so stir occasionally to ensure it doesn't stick to the bottom of the pot and burn.

Stir in the coconut milk, condensed milk, vanilla, cinnamon, nutmeg, and salt. Simmer for another 10 minutes so the spices can flavor the porridge and the mixture doesn't taste too starchy.

If the porridge seems too thick, add more water until you reach the desired consistency. If it's not sweet enough, add more condensed milk (or your preferred sweetener).

Remove from the heat. Serve hot and enjoy.

Store leftovers in an airtight container in the fridge for up to 2 days. Reheat in the microwave or in a small saucepan over low heat. You may need to add a splash of water to help loosen the porridge.

HOMINY CORN PORRIDGE

Serves 4

1 cup (160 g) dried hominy corn kernels, soaked overnight and drained

2 tablespoons light brown sugar, plus more to taste

1 cinnamon stick

½ teaspoon kosher salt

One 14-ounce (400 ml) can coconut milk (1¾ cups)

2 tablespoons cornstarch

¼ to ½ cup (60 to 125 ml) sweetened condensed milk

1 tablespoon pure vanilla extract

½ teaspoon freshly grated nutmeg

In a large saucepan, combine 6 cups (1.5 L) water with the drained hominy, the brown sugar, cinnamon stick, and salt. Bring to a boil over medium-high heat and cook until the kernels are soft enough to crush with a fork, about 30 minutes.

In a separate bowl, mix some of the coconut milk with the cornstarch to form a slurry. Add the slurry and the rest of the coconut milk to the pot, stirring to prevent lumps.

Stir in the condensed milk, vanilla, and nutmeg. Taste and adjust the sweetness as desired. Reduce the heat to medium and let simmer until the porridge thickens, about 10 minutes. If the porridge is too thick, add more water or coconut milk until you reach the desired consistency.

Remove the pot from the heat and let it sit uncovered for 5 minutes. Remove the cinnamon stick before serving.

Store leftovers in an airtight container in the fridge for up to 2 days. Reheat in the microwave or in a small saucepan over low heat. You may need to add a splash of water to help loosen the porridge.

COCO BREAD

Makes 8 rolls

One ¼-ounce envelope active dry yeast (2¼ teaspoons)

1 cup (250 ml) warm milk or coconut milk

⅓ cup (65 g) sugar

3½ cups (440 g) all-purpose flour, plus more as needed

2 teaspoons kosher salt

8 ounces (225 g) unsalted butter, melted

This simple bread is a cultural icon that connects Jamaicans from all walks of life: Everyone from the day laborer to the CEO will wrap a coco bread around a Jamaican Patty (page 40) for a satisfying, delicious lunch on the go. Best when it's fresh out of the oven, coco bread is perfect for a Fried Plantain and Egg Sandwich (page 90) or an Escovitch Fish Sandwich (page 215).

Sprinkle the yeast into a small bowl. Add the warm milk and sugar. Set aside to allow the yeast to activate, about 5 minutes. Line a baking sheet with parchment paper.

In a stand mixer bowl (or in a large bowl), combine the flour and salt.

Once the yeast mixture is slightly frothy, add it to the flour, along with ⅓ cup (75 g) of the melted butter. Stir to combine.

Snap on the dough hook and knead for 3 minutes, until the dough is soft and smooth (or knead the dough by hand for 5 minutes). The dough will be sticky at first. If it is too sticky, add more flour, 1 tablespoon at a time, as needed, until the dough easily releases from the sides of the bowl.

Divide the dough into 8 equal portions. Use a digital kitchen scale for precision, if you like. Roll each piece into a ball, then, using a rolling pin, roll each dough ball into a disk about ¼ inch (6 mm) thick. Brush with a generous amount of melted butter and fold in half, so the buttered area is inside. Place the coco breads on the parchment-lined sheet pan 2 inches (5 cm) apart. Cover the sheet pan with a damp kitchen towel and let the dough rest for 30 minutes in a warm spot.

Preheat the oven to 350°F (180°C).

Bake the coco breads for 20 minutes, or until the tops are golden. Remove from the oven and brush the tops with the remaining melted butter.

Let the coco breads cool (if you can resist the temptation) and enjoy them on their own or use them as sandwich bases. Store leftovers in an airtight container in the freezer for up to 6 months.

THE OG JAMAICAN BREAKFAST

ACKEE AND SALTFISH, FRIED DUMPLINGS, AND STEAMED CALLALOO

Ackee and saltfish, fried dumplings (Jamaicans call them johnny cakes), and sautéed callaloo: This is the holy trinity of breakfasts on the island. The three dishes complement one another perfectly in flavor and texture: buttery ackee mingling with salty cod, crispy fried dumplings, and earthy greens bursting with nutrients, all spiced up with a hint of Scotch bonnet. This meal is a filling, savory dish with ingredients that come from all over, just like the people of Jamaica. For the perfect finish, grab a slice of Toto (page 98) and pour a cup of freshly brewed Blue Mountain coffee.

ACKEE *and* SALTFISH

Serves 6

- 3 tablespoons extra-virgin olive oil
- 1 small onion, finely diced
- ½ green bell pepper, finely diced
- 2 scallions, sliced
- Leaves from 2 thyme sprigs
- ¼ to ½ Scotch bonnet pepper, minced
- 1 garlic clove, minced
- 8 ounces (225 g) boneless salt cod, prepared (see page 46)
- 1 Roma tomato, finely chopped

Heat the oil in a large skillet over medium-high heat until hot. Add the onion, bell pepper, scallions, thyme, Scotch bonnet, and garlic. Cook until the onions and peppers have softened, about 3 minutes.

Add the prepared cod and the tomatoes and cook until the tomatoes soften, about 2 minutes.

Add the ackee and stir gently to combine everything, being careful not to mash the pieces of ackee. Reduce the heat to low, cover, and simmer for 5 minutes to warm through.

Season to taste with salt and pepper. Serve immediately with fried dumplings and steamed callaloo, or on its own if you wish. Store leftovers in an airtight container in the fridge for up to 3 days.

NOTE: If you have access to fresh ackee and you know how to prepare it correctly, feel free to substitute it for the canned ackee.

One 19-ounce (540 g) can ackee, drained and rinsed (see Note)

Kosher salt and freshly ground black pepper

VARIATION

Vegetarian Ackee: To make this vegetarian, omit the salt cod and add extra vegetables. Taste it before serving; you may want to add a bit more salt.

FRIED DUMPLINGS

Makes about 12 dumplings

2½ cups (310 g) all-purpose flour, sifted

3 tablespoons sugar

1 tablespoon baking powder

1 teaspoon kosher salt

2 tablespoons (1 ounce/30 g) cold butter, cut into small pieces

½ cup (125 ml) whole milk

Vegetable oil or other neutral oil, for deep-frying

In a medium bowl, combine the flour, sugar, baking powder, and salt. Add the cold butter and use a fork or your fingers to break the butter into the flour mixture until it resembles bread crumbs. Add the milk and ¼ cup (60 ml) water and stir with a wooden spoon to combine.

Once the mixture is fully combined and sticky, use your hands to knead the dough together until it is smooth and soft, about 5 minutes, being careful not to overwork it. It should resemble pizza dough. If it's too sticky, add a little more flour. If it's too dry, add a little more water or milk. Cover the dough with a kitchen towel or plastic wrap and let it rest in the fridge for at least 30 minutes.

Line a plate with paper towels and set it near the stove. Pour 3 inches (7.5 cm) of vegetable oil into a medium saucepan and heat over medium heat to 325°F (165°C), or until the oil sizzles around a wooden spoon when it's dipped in the hot oil.

Working in batches to avoid overcrowding (these dumplings will almost double in size when fried), pinch off a piece of dough, roll into a 2-inch (5 cm) ball, and drop in the hot oil. Fry until golden brown on all sides and cooked through, turning regularly, about 10 minutes. With a slotted spoon, transfer the fried dumplings to the paper towels to drain.

Serve immediately. Fried dumplings taste best the day they are made.

recipes continue

STEAMED CALLALOO

Serves 6

2 tablespoons extra-virgin olive oil

½ onion, finely diced

1 garlic clove, thinly sliced

Leaves from 2 thyme sprigs

8 ounces (225 g) chopped callaloo (see Notes), fresh or frozen

1 Roma tomato, roughly chopped

2 scallions, thinly sliced

2 tablespoons (1 ounce/30 g) cold butter

Kosher salt and freshly ground black pepper

Heat the olive oil in a medium skillet over medium heat. Add the onion, garlic, and thyme and cook until the onions are fragrant and begin to soften, about 2 minutes.

Add the callaloo, tomato, and scallions. Stir, cover, and cook until the callaloo is wilted and tender, about 5 minutes.

Stir in the cold butter and season to taste with salt and pepper. Serve immediately (preferably with ackee and saltfish and fried dumplings).

Store leftovers in an airtight container in the fridge overnight. Heat them up in a pan with olive oil or butter for a delicious breakfast the next day.

NOTES

- If using frozen callaloo, thaw it in the fridge overnight and drain the excess liquid before using. If using fresh callaloo, wash it thoroughly before using.
- You can also use canned callaloo for this recipe—you can find this in the international aisle of most supermarkets. To use canned callaloo, drain the can and add the greens to the recipe as usual. You may not need to add salt to the recipe if using canned callaloo.
- If you can't find callaloo at all, use fresh kale—remove the stems and midribs, thinly slice, and use in the recipe in place of callaloo.

Clockwise from left to right: Steamed Callaloo, Ackee and Saltfish, and Fried Dumplings

MACKEREL RUNDOWN *with* BOILED DUMPLINGS

Serves 4

2 pounds (900 g) salted mackerel, rinsed thoroughly

For the dumplings

Kosher salt

2 cups (250 g) all-purpose flour

½ cup (80 g) fine yellow cornmeal

For the rundown

2 tablespoons coconut or extra-virgin olive oil

½ medium yellow onion, thinly sliced

2 scallions, sliced

½ Roma tomato, diced

¼ red bell pepper, sliced

¼ yellow bell pepper, sliced

3 garlic cloves, sliced

½ Scotch bonnet pepper, seeded and thinly sliced

Leaves from 3 thyme sprigs

One 14-ounce (400 ml) can coconut milk (1¾ cups)

1 teaspoon allspice berries

½ teaspoon freshly ground black pepper

½ teaspoon all-purpose seasoning, homemade (page 314) or store-bought

Kosher salt

Salted mackerel rundown (aka *run dung*) is a classic Jamaican breakfast. The traditional way of preparing it involves breaking down a fresh coconut and cooking the milk for hours to get the creaminess just right. The method used here is a bit of a cheat because it uses canned coconut milk instead, but it still results in a rich and savory sauce. My grandmother cooked mackerel rundown when the pantry got low, and somehow it always seemed to stretch to feed the entire family.

Add the rinsed mackerel to a large pot of water and bring to a boil over high heat. Boil for 5 minutes to remove the excess salt. Taste the mackerel after you've boiled it; if the fish is still too salty, boil it in a fresh pot of water for another 5 minutes over high heat, then drain and let cool slightly. Using a butter knife or your hands, remove the silver skin and carefully remove the flesh from the bones. Set aside.

Make the dumplings: Bring a large pot of salted water to a boil over high heat.

Meanwhile, in a bowl, combine the flour, cornmeal, and 1 tablespoon kosher salt. Add 1 cup (250 ml) water and mix with a spoon. Once the dough starts to come together, use your hands to knead it in the bowl for 2 minutes, until smooth.

Pinch off pieces of the dough and shape them into 3-inch (7.5 cm) disks. Gently drop the dumplings into the boiling water and cook until they all float to the top and are cooked through, about 20 minutes. Scoop the dumplings out of the boiling water with a slotted spoon or spider.

Meanwhile, make the rundown: Heat a large skillet over high heat. Add the oil, onion, scallions, tomato, red and yellow bell peppers, garlic, Scotch bonnet, and thyme. Cook, stirring occasionally, until the vegetables have softened and are fragrant, 3 to 5 minutes.

recipe continues

JAMAICA

Add the coconut milk and allspice berries and cook until reduced to a thick custard-like sauce, 6 to 8 minutes. It's okay if the sauce separates during cooking.

Add the mackerel and season with the black pepper, all-purpose seasoning, and salt to taste. Reduce the heat to low and cook for another 4 to 6 minutes so that the mackerel and the sauce can get to know each other. Remove the allspice berries before serving.

Serve the mackerel alongside the dumplings, so every bite can be a little bit of both.

NOTE: Save any leftover boiled dumplings in the fridge to make fried boiled dumplings the next day. To do so, heat 1 inch (2.5 cm) of vegetable oil in a sauté pan over medium-high heat and fry the boiled dumplings until golden brown, about 4 minutes on either side. These are delicious with leftover mackerel rundown.

CLASSIC JAMAICAN BREAKFAST SIDES

The traditional Jamaican breakfast was designed to fuel a hard day's work on the land, back when my ancestors grew their food on the provision ground. These were small plots with the worst soil, set aside for enslaved people to cultivate, to save plantation owners the cost of feeding them. The foods that grew well in this poor soil are still a big part of the Jamaican diet: yams, cassava, sweet potatoes, and taro, among others. We call them ground provisions, hard food, or just *food*, and a traditional Jamaican breakfast usually includes at least one.

Ground provisions are starchy vegetables and tubers that are boiled and served alongside main dishes like Ackee and Saltfish (page 78) and Mackerel Rundown (page 82). Here are some of the most popular ground provisions:

Yam: Not to be confused with the sweet potato (see page 119), yam is a starchy tuber with a firm texture and a slightly sweet taste.

Green banana: These unripe bananas have a starchy, potato-like texture and are boiled for a versatile side that complements many dishes.

Dasheen (taro): This root vegetable is similar to yam and has a slightly nutty flavor.

Breadfruit: This starchy fruit grows on large trees and has a bready flavor and texture when roasted or fried.

BREAKFAST ROTI BURRITOS

Serves 4

For the roti

2 cups (250 g) all-purpose flour, plus more for dusting

2 teaspoons sugar

2 teaspoons baking powder

2 teaspoons kosher salt

1 cup (250 ml) warm water

1 tablespoon extra-virgin olive oil

8 tablespoons (4 ounces/115 g) butter or ghee, at room temperature

For the burritos

2 tablespoons extra-virgin olive oil

1 red bell pepper, sliced

½ large yellow onion, sliced

2 garlic cloves, minced

8 ounces (225 g) fresh chorizo

6 large eggs, beaten

2 avocados, sliced

½ cup (55 g) shredded Cheddar cheese

Hot sauce (optional), for serving

Caribbean cuisine is an amazing fusion of flavors from many cultures. Roti, introduced by indentured laborers from India in the early nineteenth century, is a versatile flatbread perfect for sopping up curry or dipping in stews. In this recipe, it wraps around a hearty filling of chorizo, avocado, cheese, and scrambled eggs, creating a breakfast burrito that will get you through the morning and then some. Serve these burritos with hot sauce for an extra kick.

Make the roti: In a large bowl, combine the flour, sugar, baking powder, and salt and mix well with a wooden spoon. Add the water and olive oil and combine until a sticky dough forms. Knead the dough in the bowl until it's soft and smooth but still slightly sticky, about 1 minute. If the dough is too sticky, add another 1 to 2 tablespoons of flour, mixing until it comes together.

Turn the dough out onto a lightly floured work surface and knead for 2 minutes, until smooth. Divide the dough into 4 equal portions, then roll each into a ball and cover them with a clean, damp kitchen towel. Let them rest for 15 minutes at room temperature.

Uncover, sprinkle flour onto a work surface, and use a rolling pin to roll each ball of dough into a round ¼ inch (6 mm) thick.

Rub 1 tablespoon of the softened butter onto the surface of each round of dough with your fingers. Then cut a slit from the center to the outer edge of each round. Starting from the slit side, roll each round of dough into a cone. Push the pointed end into the middle a bit, as if to squish it down (see page 88). Cover the dough with a clean, damp kitchen towel and let rest for another 30 minutes.

Heat a cast-iron skillet or a griddle over medium heat. While the pan heats, flatten each piece of dough with your hands. On a lightly floured work surface, using a rolling pin, roll each piece of dough out into a 12-inch (30 cm) round about ¼ inch (6 mm) thick.

recipe continues

Gently place one round of dough in the skillet and brush a generous amount of the remaining butter or ghee onto the side facing up. Cook the dough until bubbles start to form in the roti, 2 to 3 minutes. Gently flip the dough with a spatula and cook until the other side is golden brown, another 1 to 2 minutes. Repeat the process until all four roti are cooked. If there's any butter or ghee left over, brush the tops of the rotis with it. Stack the rotis on a plate and cover with a clean kitchen towel.

Make the burritos: Set the same skillet over medium-high heat. Add the olive oil, bell pepper, onion, and garlic and cook, stirring frequently, until the onions and peppers are fragrant and beginning to caramelize around the edges, 3 to 5 minutes.

Reduce the heat to medium, add the chorizo to the pan, and cook, stirring frequently, until the chorizo is fully cooked, about 5 minutes.

Move the chorizo mix to one side of the skillet and pour the whisked eggs into the other side. Cook, stirring constantly with a silicone spatula, until the eggs are cooked through but not dried out, about 2 minutes. Remove from the heat.

To assemble the breakfast burritos, lay each roti on a cutting board or plate. Top each roti with some of the chorizo mix, scrambled eggs, avocado slices, and some shredded Cheddar. Wrap each one like a burrito and serve immediately with hot sauce, if desired.

NOTE: The dough for the roti can be made 1 day ahead. To do this, follow the steps up until the point of cooking the rotis. Store the dough in the fridge in an airtight container.

FRIED PLANTAIN AND EGG SANDWICHES

Makes 4 sandwiches

One 12-ounce (340 g) package bacon

1 large ripe plantain, sliced on a bias into pieces ½ inch (2.5 cm) thick

4 large eggs

Kosher salt and freshly ground black pepper

4 Coco Breads (page 76) or your favorite rolls, warmed

1 beefsteak tomato, thinly sliced

Lettuce (any type you have on hand)

Crispy bacon, sweet ripe plantain, and the richness of a fried egg wrapped in freshly baked coco bread make this sandwich unforgettable. Add a slice of cheese for added creaminess or a drizzle of hot sauce for a bit of heat. You can even switch out the coco bread for your favorite type of roll or bread if you don't feel like baking.

Preheat the oven to 400°F (200°C). Line a sheet pan with parchment paper or foil. Line a plate with paper towels and set it nearby.

Arrange the bacon in a single layer on the prepared sheet pan. Bake for 10 to 20 minutes, depending on your preference for bacon crispness, then transfer the bacon to the paper towels to drain.

Pour the bacon fat from the sheet pan into a bowl and set it aside for frying the plantain and the eggs. If there are a lot of crispy bits in the fat, strain before using.

Line a second plate with paper towels and set it near the stove. Heat half of the bacon fat in a large skillet over medium heat. Add the sliced plantain and fry until golden, about 3 minutes on each side. Keep a close eye on it while frying—ripe plantain burns easily because of its high sugar content. Transfer the plantain slices to the paper towels to drain.

Add the rest of the bacon fat to the same pan, still over medium heat. Crack the eggs into the pan and cook until the whites are opaque and the yolks just start to set around the edges, 2 to 3 minutes (see Note). Season the eggs with a sprinkle of salt and pepper.

Once the eggs are cooked, open each coco bread and assemble the sandwiches with a couple of pieces each of bacon, plantain, tomato, and lettuce. Top with an egg, close, and enjoy immediately.

NOTE: If you don't like your eggs sunny-side up with a slightly runny yolk, cook them a little longer, or flip them gently for over-easy eggs.

COCONUT BANANA PANCAKES

Makes 12 pancakes

- 2 ripe bananas, mashed
- One 14-ounce (400 ml) can coconut milk (1¾ cups)
- 3 tablespoons (1.5 ounces/45 g) unsalted butter, melted
- 2 tablespoons light brown sugar
- 2 large eggs, beaten
- 2 teaspoons pure vanilla extract
- 2 cups (250 g) all-purpose flour
- ½ cup (40 g) sweetened shredded coconut
- 1 tablespoon baking powder
- ½ teaspoon kosher salt
- ½ teaspoon ground cinnamon
- ½ teaspoon freshly grated nutmeg
- Vegetable oil or other neutral oil, for cooking
- Pancake syrup, for serving
- Sliced banana, for serving

You won't find pancakes on a traditional Jamaican breakfast menu, but locals have developed quite a fondness for them. This recipe infuses island flavors into the classic American dish, perfectly blending the two cultures. Your kitchen will smell like the Caribbean with the scents of banana, vanilla, cinnamon, and nutmeg.

In a medium bowl, combine the mashed bananas, coconut milk, melted butter, brown sugar, eggs, and vanilla.

In a large bowl, mix the flour, coconut, baking powder, salt, cinnamon, and nutmeg.

Add the banana mixture to the flour mixture and stir with a silicone spatula until combined.

Preheat the oven to 250°F (120°C).

Heat a large nonstick griddle or skillet over medium-low heat for about 5 minutes. Add about 2 tablespoons oil to the pan. Scoop ¼ cup (60 ml) of batter into the pan. Repeat, being careful not to overcrowd the pan.

Once the pancakes begin to form bubbles on the surface and the edges have started to brown lightly, about 4 minutes, flip and cook until the other side is golden brown, about 3 minutes. Transfer the pancakes to a sheet pan and place in the warmed oven until ready to serve. Repeat the process until you've used all the batter.

Serve warm with pancake syrup and sliced bananas.

BEST BANANA BREAD

Makes 1 loaf

Softened butter, for the pan

4 to 5 large ripe bananas, mashed (about 2 cups/450 g)

2 large eggs, lightly beaten

½ cup (110 g) packed light brown sugar

½ cup (100 g) granulated sugar

8 tablespoons (4 ounces/115 g) unsalted butter, melted

¼ cup (60 ml) vegetable oil or other neutral oil

1 tablespoon pure vanilla extract

1 teaspoon almond extract (optional)

1½ cups (190 g) all-purpose flour

1 teaspoon baking soda

1 teaspoon ground cinnamon

½ teaspoon freshly grated nutmeg

½ teaspoon kosher salt

For the topping

¼ cup (30 g) all-purpose flour

¼ cup (55 g) packed light brown sugar

¼ cup (30 g) chopped walnuts

4 tablespoons (2 ounces/60 g) unsalted butter, melted

1 teaspoon ground cinnamon

¼ teaspoon kosher salt

You can make this recipe in no time and it doesn't even require a stand mixer, so cleanup is easy too. The most difficult part is waiting for the bananas to ripen. Enjoy banana bread alongside the OG Jamaican Breakfast (page 78) or with a steaming mug of tea or cocoa before breakfast to, as we say at home, "buss gas" (get rid of hunger pangs).

Preheat the oven to 350°F (180°C). Grease a 9-by-5-inch (23 by 13 cm) nonstick loaf pan with butter.

In a large bowl, combine the mashed bananas, eggs, brown sugar, granulated sugar, melted butter, oil, vanilla, and almond extract (if using). Whisk until combined.

In a medium bowl, sift together the flour, baking soda, cinnamon, nutmeg, and salt.

Add the spiced flour mixture to the banana mixture and mix with a spatula until combined. Pour the batter into the greased loaf pan.

Make the topping: In a small bowl, mix the flour, brown sugar, walnuts, melted butter, cinnamon, and salt. Spread the mixture evenly over the top of the banana bread batter and gently press it in.

Bake for about 1 hour, or until the bread is golden brown and a toothpick inserted in the center comes out clean. If the top starts to brown too much before the middle is cooked, cover with foil and continue baking until done.

Remove the loaf from the pan and set it on a cooling rack until it's cool enough to handle. Slice into thick pieces and enjoy. Store leftovers in an airtight container at room temperature for up to 3 days.

VARIATIONS

Loaded Banana Bread: If you wish, mix ½ cup walnuts, pecans, raisins, or chocolate chips into the batter.

Best Banana Muffins: Want muffins instead? The recipe yields 12 muffins. Bake for 25 to 30 minutes.

COCO-COFFEE GRANOLA

Makes about 2 quarts (2 L) granola

- 2 tablespoons instant coffee powder
- 1 tablespoon boiling water
- 4 cups (320 g) rolled oats
- ½ cup (50 g) sliced almonds
- ½ cup (75 g) whole cashews
- ½ cup (60 g) pumpkin seeds
- ¼ cup (15 g) unsweetened cocoa powder
- 2 tablespoons flaxseeds
- 2 tablespoons chia seeds
- 1 teaspoon kosher salt
- 1 teaspoon ground cinnamon
- ½ cup (125 ml) honey or maple syrup
- ½ cup (110 g) coconut oil, melted
- 1 teaspoon pure vanilla extract
- 1 cup (85 g) unsweetened coconut flakes, toasted lightly (see Note, page 55)

This granola brings a taste of the Caribbean to a Western-style breakfast, with a rich blend of coffee and cocoa alongside tropical flavors like coconut and cinnamon. It's packed with grains, nuts, and seeds for a satisfying, energizing start to the day. Whether layered with yogurt or sprinkled over fruit, it's a reminder that Caribbean ingredients are perfect for all kinds of breakfasts.

Preheat the oven to 350°F (180°C). Line a large sheet pan with parchment paper.

In a small bowl, mix the instant coffee powder and boiling water. Set aside.

In a large bowl, combine the oats, almonds, cashews, pumpkin seeds, cocoa powder, flaxseeds, chia seeds, salt, and cinnamon and stir to combine. Pour in the honey, melted coconut oil, vanilla, and coffee mixture and mix until the dry ingredients are fully coated.

Pour the mixture onto the prepared pan and use a spatula to spread it evenly around the pan, pressing down lightly.

Bake until lightly golden, 20 to 25 minutes, stirring halfway through and pressing the granola down with the spatula after stirring.

Remove the granola from the oven and let cool fully in the pan. Do not stir the granola until it has fully cooled. Once it's cooled, break the granola apart with your hands or stir with a spoon, keeping plenty of clumps together. Gently toss in the toasted coconut.

Store in an airtight container at room temperature for up to 2 weeks or in the freezer for up to 3 months.

TOTO (COCONUT CAKE)

Makes one 9-inch (23 cm) square loaf

- 1 cup (220 g) packed light brown sugar
- ¾ cup (6 ounces/170 g) unsalted butter, melted
- One 14-ounce (400 ml) can coconut milk (1¾ cups)
- 2 large eggs, beaten
- 1 teaspoon grated orange zest
- 1 teaspoon pure vanilla extract
- ½ teaspoon almond extract
- 2 cups (250 g) all-purpose flour
- 1 tablespoon baking powder
- 1 teaspoon ground cinnamon
- ½ teaspoon freshly grated nutmeg
- ½ teaspoon kosher salt
- 1 cup (85 g) sweetened shredded coconut

Welcome to a slice of sweetness from Jamaica's rich culinary heritage. This comforting, dense cake emerged from the struggles of the island's plantation days. The original version was a humble dish, made with the simple but enduring ingredients of flour, coconut, and molasses. Today, Jamaicans enjoy toto as an easy, convenient breakfast or snack. It's quick to bake and perfect for busy mornings.

Preheat the oven to 350°F (180°C). Line a 9-inch (23 cm) square baking pan with parchment paper.

In a large bowl, whisk together the brown sugar and melted butter. Add the coconut milk, eggs, orange zest, vanilla, and almond extract. Mix until combined.

In a medium bowl, sift the flour, baking powder, cinnamon, nutmeg, and salt through a fine-mesh sieve.

Add the flour mixture to the wet ingredients and mix with a silicone spatula until the batter just comes together. Fold in the shredded coconut. Pour the batter into the prepared pan.

Bake for 40 minutes, or until a toothpick comes out clean when inserted in the center.

Let cool in the pan on a wire rack. Once the cake is completely cooled, lift it out of the pan by the parchment.

Store in an airtight container or wrapped tightly in plastic wrap in the fridge for up to 1 week.

ONE POT, FULL FLAVOR

SOUP SATURDAY

The aroma of Satdeh *soup—chicken, beef, goat, fish, red peas, whatever is in season—fills houses and spills into streets and alleyways all around Jamaica on the weekend. Soup is flexible, easy to make, and a great budget-stretcher. Good soup fills, nourishes, and comforts. And when it's 96 degrees in the shade? Hot soup is still the answer.*

Soup essentials include Soup Seasoning, dumplings, pumpkin (for its gorgeous color and full flavor), some kind of ground provision (what Jamaicans call simply *food*), and a few hours to watch the pot. Extra time intensifies the flavors and thickens the broth, making most of these soups, like Ital-Style Red Peas Soup and Jamaican Chicken Soup, heavy and satisfying enough to be a whole meal. If you're more in the mood for something light and refreshing, try Carrot-Ginger Soup.

ITAL-STYLE RED PEAS SOUP

Serves 6 to 8

2 cups (370 g) dried kidney beans (see Note)

5 garlic cloves, smashed and peeled

4 thyme sprigs

1 teaspoon allspice berries or ½ teaspoon ground allspice

One 14-ounce (400 ml) can coconut milk or (1¾ cups)

1 onion, diced

½ Scotch bonnet pepper, chopped

1 tablespoon vegetable bouillon paste

2 teaspoons kosher salt, plus more to taste

½ teaspoon grated fresh ginger

8 ounces (225 g) yellow yam (see page 119), peeled and cut into 1-inch (2.5 cm) cubes

3 scallions, sliced

2 medium carrots, diced

1 chayote or 1 Yukon Gold potato, peeled and cut into 1-inch (2.5 cm) cubes

Spinners (recipe follows)

Freshly ground black pepper

Ital is a key pillar of Rastafari, the Jamaican-grown religion with over a million followers worldwide. It's about living a pure and natural lifestyle, in part by eating a plant-based diet of foods that are natural, whole, unprocessed, and free from salt, additives, and chemicals. Rastafarians are the original vegans. Though this recipe is not fully Ital (because it uses store-bought bouillon and canned coconut milk), it still pays homage to an essential part of Jamaica's culinary legacy. The coconut, red peas, allspice, and Scotch bonnet blend to create what is almost a sweetness in this dish, delivering a uniquely Jamaican punch of velvety, fragrant goodness. Like its cousin Stew Peas (page 165), this soup is a rugged staple in Jamaican cooking. You will need to start this recipe a day in advance to give the kidney beans time to soak.

In a large pot, combine 10 cups (2.4 L) water and the kidney beans and let the beans soak, covered, for at least 5 hours or overnight. Do not discard the soaking water, as this is what will give the soup a beautiful mahogany color.

Once the beans have soaked, add the garlic, thyme sprigs, and allspice berries to the pot and bring to a boil over high heat. Reduce the heat to medium, cover, and cook at a rapid simmer until the beans are tender, 50 to 60 minutes. Discard the thyme sprigs and allspice berries.

Add the coconut milk, onion, Scotch bonnet, bouillon paste, salt, and ginger and bring to a simmer over medium heat. Cook for 10 minutes to allow the flavors to come together, then add the yam, scallions, carrots, chayote, and spinners and continue to cook until the vegetables are tender and the spinners float to the surface of the soup, another 20 minutes.

recipe continues

Season to taste with salt and freshly ground pepper. If you prefer a thinner soup, add another cup or two of water and simmer for another 5 minutes before serving.

Store leftovers in an airtight container in the fridge for up to 4 days or in the freezer for up to 3 months; the spinners will be less dense once thawed and reheated.

NOTE: You can use canned kidney beans if you don't have time to soak the beans. To substitute canned beans, use two 15.5-ounce (439 g) cans of kidney beans (liquid included). Cook the beans with 8 cups (2 L) of water and the garlic, thyme, and allspice berries for 15 minutes, then continue to follow the recipe as written.

VARIATION

Add pig's tail or beef stew meat for extra protein and flavor. See Stew Peas with Pig's Tail (page 165) for tips on how to work with pig's tail.

Spinners

Makes 12 to 18 spinners

1 cup (125 g) all-purpose flour

½ teaspoon kosher salt

In a small bowl, mix the flour and salt together. Add ¼ cup (60 ml) water and combine with a spoon.

Once the dough starts to come together, use your hands to knead it for 2 minutes, until smooth. If the flour doesn't fully incorporate, add more water a tablespoon at a time (but no more than another ¼ cup/60 ml) and knead until smooth. Pinch off small pieces of the dough—roughly the size of the tip of your thumb—and shape them into small fingerlike dumplings or disks.

Add the raw spinners to hot soup. They are ready to eat when they float to the top.

HOW TO MAKE COCONUT MILK AT HOME

Making fresh, authentic coconut milk is truly a labor of love, but it's worth it for a special occasion. Coconuts are readily available at most grocery stores. Choose coconuts that feel heavy for their size and are free of visible cracks. To open the coconut, use a heavy tool like a cleaver or hammer over a bowl to catch the coconut water (which goes very well with rum on ice, by the way). Pry the coconut meat from the shell with a strong, sharp knife (preferably one with a curved edge, like a paring knife, steak knife, or even a butter knife) and rinse it to remove any shell fragments. To make the milk, you can use either of the methods below.

Old-School Method: Grate the coconut meat with the small-hole shredder side of a box grater. Add the grated meat to a bowl with warm water (about 4 cups/1 L per 2 coconuts) and let sit for 10 minutes. Knead and squeeze the grated coconut to extract the milk. Pour the mixture through a cheesecloth into another bowl, squeezing to get all the milk out.

Blender Method: Cut the coconut meat into small pieces and blend it with water (about 4 cups/1 L per 2 coconuts) until smooth. Pour the mixture through a cheesecloth into a bowl, squeezing to extract the milk.

Store fresh coconut milk in an airtight container in the fridge for up to 4 days. Shake well before using, as it may separate.

JAMAICAN CHICKEN SOUP

Serves 6 to 8

8 cups (2 L) chicken stock (see Note)

1½ pounds (680 g) boneless, skinless chicken thighs, cut into 1-inch (2.5 cm) chunks

1 pound (450 g) Jamaican pumpkin (calabaza squash), peeled and cut into large chunks

1 medium onion, diced

Leaves from 6 thyme sprigs

4 garlic cloves, sliced

½ teaspoon ground allspice

2 carrots, chopped

2 ears corn, shucked and cut into quarters

1 chayote, peeled and cut into 1-inch (2.5 cm) pieces

2 yellow potatoes, peeled and cut into 1-inch (2.5 cm) pieces

1 Scotch bonnet pepper, left whole

¼ cup (70 g) Soup Seasoning (page 311) or a store-bought soup mix like Grace Cock Soup

Spinners (page 106)

4 scallions, sliced

Kosher salt and freshly ground black pepper

This soup is one of the best meals you can make in less than 45 minutes. Traditionally prepared with chicken feet or bone-in chicken to create an intense bone broth base, this version uses chicken stock and homemade seasoning to produce the soup's trademark flavor bomb. Pumpkin is crucial to this soup, adding gorgeous color, hearty texture, and earthy flavor. Spinners (small flour dumplings) and Scotch bonnet pepper add texture and a hint of heat. Unlike typical lighter chicken soups, this Jamaican chicken soup is a robust, filling meal in a bowl.

In a large pot, combine the chicken stock, chicken thighs, pumpkin, onion, thyme, garlic, and allspice. Bring to a boil over high heat, then cover and cook at a rapid boil until the pumpkin breaks down, about 20 minutes. If the pumpkin doesn't naturally break down after this time, break up the pieces with a fork.

Stir in the carrots, corn, chayote, potatoes, Scotch bonnet, and soup seasoning. Reduce the heat to medium-high and continue cooking until the carrots, chayote, and potatoes are tender, about 15 minutes.

Reduce the heat to medium and add the spinners and scallions to the pot. Cook, uncovered, until the spinners rise to the top and are cooked through, about 10 minutes.

Season to taste with salt and pepper. Discard the Scotch bonnet before serving.

Store leftovers in an airtight container in the fridge for 3 to 5 days or in the freezer for up to 3 months. The spinners will be less dense once the soup is thawed and reheated.

NOTE: In place of the chicken stock, you can use bouillon cubes or paste dissolved in water.

MY GRANDMOTHER'S HANDS

Veronica Eulalee Davis was known to most people as Miss Cherry. To me and my siblings she was Mama Cherry—grandmother, teacher, parent.

At our house, Satdeh soup hinged on what was left in the pantry at the end of the week: half a cho-cho, a yam, a piece of pumpkin, maybe a bit of pig's tail if we were lucky. But long before the soup went on the fire, Mama Cherry made a pot of coffee to tell me it was time to get up. And if the shriek of the kettle didn't wake me, the steaming hot coffee under my nose did. I stumbled out of bed, splashed cold water on my face, and followed her out the door.

I loved Coronation Market: bins and boxes piled high with mangoes, carrots, plantain. Each vendor louder than the last. "Peanut, peanut, peanut!" a woman shouted over the crowd. We always got there early to beat the traffic and the mayhem and to make sure we got the freshest produce. I was in awe of how Mama Cherry navigated the maze of vendors, weaving this way and that to get from her onion lady to her tomato man to the boy selling little bags of hot peppers, pausing only long enough to make sure I was still behind her.

An hour later we were done, our bags bulging with onions, flour, thyme, and scallions, or maybe beef bones, tomatoes, and cassava. We rushed home to start the soup.

I watched in the kitchen as Mama Cherry's weathered hands guided a cascade of dried red kidney beans into an old pot. They made a soft clinking sound as she washed and picked through them, carefully removing tiny stones and sticks and other bits that didn't belong. She would tell me, "Every day when yuh get up, Andre, try do one thing a likkle better." Her voice was warm, but her words carried the weight of her experience and the hardships that defined her life. I'd nod and we'd revert to silence, except for the tinny radio crackling from the next room. Mama Cherry's hands moved smoothly as she added water, tossed in garlic, pimento, and a few sprigs of thyme, then covered the pot and set it on the coal fire.

Once the peas had softened, Mama Cherry added the rest of the seasonings—more thyme, Scotch bonnet, scallions. Still later, she would taste the thick broth and hold out the wooden spoon for me to try it.

Tasting often was how I learned from Mama Cherry to layer flavors in even the simplest dishes. Making Satdeh soup came to me by osmosis. There was no cookbook, just my grandmother's hands and her gentle guidance.

BIG

FISH TEA

Serves 4 to 6

8 ounces (225 g) Jamaican pumpkin (calabaza squash), peeled and cubed

1 onion, finely diced

1 small cassava (yuca), about 8 ounces (225 g), peeled and cubed

1 carrot, chopped

2 fish or vegetable bouillon cubes

2 garlic cloves, minced

Leaves from 4 thyme sprigs

1 Scotch bonnet pepper, left whole

3 tablespoons Soup Seasoning (page 311) or store-bought soup mix

½ teaspoon allspice berries

1 pound (450 g) snapper fillet, cut into 1-inch (2.5 cm) cubes

8 okra pods, cut into 1-inch (2.5 cm) pieces

4 scallions, sliced

Kosher salt and freshly ground black pepper

Fish tea is not tea at all; it's soup. The name comes from its brothy consistency, which is uncommon among Jamaican soups. What it lacks in body it makes up for with its delicate, fresh ocean flavor. Fish tea uses smaller fish or the heads and tails of larger fish, reflecting Jamaica's nose-to-tail culture, where nothing goes to waste. This soup is laden with vegetables, spices, and ground provisions, perfect for a summer's evening, or when you crave something light but satisfying.

In a large pot, combine 10 cups (2.5 L) water with the pumpkin, onion, cassava, carrot, bouillon cubes, garlic, thyme, Scotch bonnet, soup seasoning, and allspice berries. Bring to a boil over medium-high heat. Reduce the heat to medium-low and cook until the vegetables begin to soften, about 20 minutes.

Add the snapper, okra, and scallions and cook until the fish is cooked through and all the vegetables are tender, about 10 minutes. Discard the allspice berries and season to taste with salt and black pepper.

Serve immediately. Store leftovers in an airtight container in the fridge for up to 2 days.

MANNISH WATER (GOAT SOUP)

Serves 8 to 10

- 2 pounds (900 g) bone-in goat meat (see Note), cut into chunks
- 8 ounces (225 g) Jamaican pumpkin (calabaza squash), peeled and cut into large chunks
- 1 onion, diced
- 6 garlic cloves, chopped
- 3 vegetable bouillon cubes
- 1 tablespoon kosher salt, plus more to taste
- 1 teaspoon grated fresh ginger
- 1 teaspoon allspice berries
- Leaves from 4 thyme sprigs
- 2 bay leaves
- 8 ounces (225 g) yellow yam, peeled and cut into 1-inch (2.5 cm) cubes
- 1 carrot, chopped
- 1 unpeeled green banana (optional), skin on, rinsed and sliced into ½-inch (1.5 cm) pieces
- 1 chayote, peeled and chopped
- 6 scallions, sliced
- 1 Scotch bonnet pepper, left whole
- 3 tablespoons Soup Seasoning (page 311) or store-bought soup mix
- ½ teaspoon freshly ground black pepper

Jamaicans don't call this dish Mannish Water for nothing. This hearty soup, famed for its "invigorating" properties, is said to put hair on your chest and pep in your step. The soup was traditionally cooked by men, outside over a wood fire, using all parts of the goat, from head to offal (including testicles) to tail. Nose-to-tail is nothing new to the island; it's so ingrained in the Jamaican way of life we don't even have a name for it. The whole-goat version of Mannish Water is rarely made at home because it's too complicated, but it's popular to serve at weddings, birthdays, and funerals. This recipe is easier and faster and uses just the goat meat. You can make substitutions for most of the ingredients, but don't use anything except Scotch bonnet pepper—its intense, fruity, knock-your-hat-off heat is the cornerstone of Jamaican cuisine.

In a large soup pot, combine 10 cups (2.5 L) water with the goat meat, pumpkin, onion, garlic, bouillon cubes, salt, ginger, allspice berries, half the thyme, and the bay leaves. Bring to a boil over high heat. Reduce the heat to medium so the liquid stays at a low boil, cover, and cook until the goat is tender and the pumpkin has broken apart, about 1½ hours.

Add 2 cups (500 ml) water along with the yam, carrot, green banana (if using), chayote, scallions, Scotch bonnet, soup seasoning, black pepper, and remaining thyme. Simmer, uncovered, over medium heat until all the vegetables are tender, about 20 minutes.

Discard the bay leaves, Scotch bonnet, and allspice berries. Season to taste with salt. Serve immediately. Store leftovers in an airtight container in the fridge for 3 days or in the freezer for up to 3 months.

NOTE: Substitute lamb stew meat if you can't find any goat meat, and feel free to use boneless goat or lamb meat if you don't like the bone-in version.

For Sale in Jamaica & The Caribbean Only
SPICY
RAM-GOAT SOUP
MANNISH WATER
NATURAL NO MSG
Net Wt. 1.76 oz (50 grams)
Soup At Its Best
RAM GOAT
PRODUCT
200 g

JAMAICAN PEPPER POT

Serves 6 to 8

1 pound (450 g) cured salt beef (see Notes), cut into 2-inch (5 cm) cubes

1 pound (450 g) beef stew meat, cut into 2-inch (5 cm) cubes

2 medium onions, diced

6 scallions, sliced

6 garlic cloves, roughly chopped

Leaves from 4 thyme sprigs

2 bay leaves

1 teaspoon allspice berries

1 teaspoon grated fresh ginger

2 beef bouillon cubes (see Notes)

One 19-ounce (540 g) can callaloo (see Notes), drained (2⅓ cups)

One 14-ounce (400 ml) can coconut milk (1¾ cups)

½ pound (225 g) yellow yam, peeled and cubed

1 small sweet potato, peeled and cut into 1-inch (2.5 cm) cubes

2 carrots, chopped

1 Scotch bonnet pepper, left whole

1 green bell pepper, finely diced

8 okra pods, cut into 1-inch (2.5 cm) pieces

Kosher salt and freshly ground black pepper

There are two different pepper pot soups in the Caribbean. One is from Guyana, and it's a meaty dish stewed for hours in a thick black sauce made from cassava root. That version of pepper pot can be traced back to the indigenous Amerindian people of Guyana. The other is a nutritious, vegetal green soup with roots in West Africa, and this one is a favorite in Jamaica. As with a lot of African dishes, precise ingredients vary depending on what's available. All Jamaicans will agree on one thing: If it doesn't include callaloo, it's not real pepper pot. Note that the cured beef needs to be soaked overnight or boiled for an hour to remove the salt, so you'll want to plan ahead.

To prepare the cured beef, soak it overnight in cold water in the fridge or boil for 1 hour to remove the salt. In either case, discard the water and rinse the cured meat under cold running water before continuing with recipe.

In a large soup pot, combine the prepared cured beef, beef stew meat, and 12 cups (2.8 L) water. Add the onions, scallions, garlic, thyme, bay leaves, allspice berries, ginger, and bouillon cubes. Bring to a boil, then reduce the heat to maintain a simmer and cook until the beef is almost tender, 1 to 1½ hours.

Remove 2 cups (500 ml) of the liquid from the pot, including some of the onions and aromatics, and place in a blender with half the callaloo. Puree the mixture and return it to the pot. (You can skip this step if you prefer a chunkier soup.)

Add the rest of the callaloo and the coconut milk, yam, sweet potato, carrots, and Scotch bonnet to the pot. Cook over medium heat until the sweet potato has cooked through, about 20 minutes.

Add the bell pepper and okra and simmer until the okra has broken down and is gummy, about 15 minutes.

recipe continues

Discard the bay leaves, Scotch bonnet, and allspice berries. Season to taste with salt and black pepper. Serve hot. Store leftovers in an airtight container in the fridge for up to 3 days.

NOTES

- Cured salt beef, also called corned beef (but not the kind in the can), is salted and cured in a nitrate solution. It is available in Jamaican and Caribbean markets in the meats/deli section.
- Depending on the salt level in the cured beef, you may want to use low-sodium or sodium-free bouillon cubes and omit the kosher salt.
- You can substitute 1 pound (450 g) fresh callaloo or fresh kale for the canned callaloo.

VARIATION

Vegan Pepper Pot: It's easy to make this vegan; just omit the meat and use vegan bouillon cubes.

NATIONAL PEPPER POT DAY

In the United States, December 29 is celebrated as National Pepper Pot Day. This day commemorates the pepper pot soup that nourished George Washington's troops during the harsh winter of 1777 at Valley Forge. It has even been called "the Soup That Saved America." While most historical records give credit to the baker general for this soup, I would bet the president's enslaved cook, Hercules Posey, was responsible. Posey was known to frequent the public market in Philadelphia, where he met and interacted with the "pepper pot women," who were of African and Caribbean descent. These women sold a rich, hearty soup made with a variety of peppers, spices, root vegetables, beef tripe, herbs, and leafy greens. The *New Art of Cookery*, published in Philadelphia in 1792, even includes a recipe for West Indian pepper pot.

A YAM IS A YAM IS A YAM (AND NOT A SWEET POTATO)

The terms *yam* and *sweet potato* have long been (mis)used interchangeably, even though they are completely different vegetables. Likewise, sweet potatoes are not related at all to regular (Irish) potatoes. True yams, native to Africa and Asia, have rough brown skin and are starchier and drier than sweet potatoes, which are moist and . . . well . . . sweet. The confusion started centuries ago when enslaved Africans brought variations of the word—*nyami, nyam, enyame*—with them to North America. It actually means "to eat," which brings us back to Jamaica, where, if you're hungry, you will "nyam" some food. The displaced Africans replaced the yams they knew with available sweet potatoes in their dishes and used their old word for the new food.

The confusion was exacerbated in the 1930s when growers in the southern United States began producing the darker-fleshed sweet potatoes. The marketers aimed to make Louisiana's sweeter, moister, orange-fleshed sweet potatoes stand out from the firmer, drier, white-fleshed varieties grown in northern regions, and the "Louisiana yam" was born. Producers and marketers eagerly adopted the idea, and now, nearly a century later, sweet potatoes are still being called "yams."

Today there are somewhere between six thousand and eight thousand varieties of sweet potatoes in cultivation around the world, and unless you look for actual yams, which can be found in many international markets, you are probably buying sweet potatoes.

CARROT-GINGER SOUP

Serves 4 to 6

2 tablespoons extra-virgin olive oil

1 medium onion, chopped

½ leek, white and light-green parts only, chopped

2 celery stalks, chopped

3 to 4 large carrots, diced (about 3 cups/545 g)

1 tablespoon minced fresh ginger

4 garlic cloves, minced

1 teaspoon smoked paprika

1 teaspoon ground turmeric

1 teaspoon ground cumin

6 cups (1.5 L) vegetable stock (see Note)

1 cup (250 ml) coconut milk

2 bay leaves

Leaves from 1 thyme sprig

¼ cup (60 ml) heavy cream (optional)

2 tablespoons (1 ounce/30 g) cold butter (optional)

Kosher salt and freshly ground black pepper

Coco Bread (page 76), for serving (optional)

This soup might not be a traditional Jamaican recipe, but it's one of my favorites. It's a healthy, vibrant dish that's easy to prepare and looks as amazing as it tastes. The bright orange from the carrots combined with the warm notes from ginger, turmeric, and cumin make it a standout at any meal. While it's perfect as a comforting bowl of soup, consider serving it as a starter to whet the appetite at your next dinner party. Pair it with coco bread for dipping or drizzle with a touch of coconut milk for a more elegant presentation.

Heat a large pot over medium heat. Pour in the olive oil and add the onion, leek, and celery. Cook until the vegetables have softened, about 5 minutes. Add the carrots, ginger, garlic, smoked paprika, turmeric, and cumin and cook, stirring occasionally, until fragrant, 2 to 3 minutes.

Add the vegetable stock, coconut milk, bay leaves, and thyme. Bring to a boil, then reduce the heat to low and simmer until the vegetables are tender, 25 to 30 minutes.

Working in two batches (or more, depending on the size of your blender), and being careful not to overfill and burn your hands, transfer the soup to a blender. Put a dish towel over the top of the blender. Start blending on low speed and gradually increase speed, then blend until smooth. For a creamier soup, add the heavy cream and butter and blend again to emulsify.

Return the pureed soup to the pot. Season to taste with salt and black pepper. Serve, with coco bread alongside if desired.

Store the soup in an airtight container in the fridge for up to 4 days or in the freezer for up to 3 months.

NOTE: You can use water and vegetable bouillon cubes or paste in place of vegetable stock.

COMPLEMENTS

SIDE DISHES

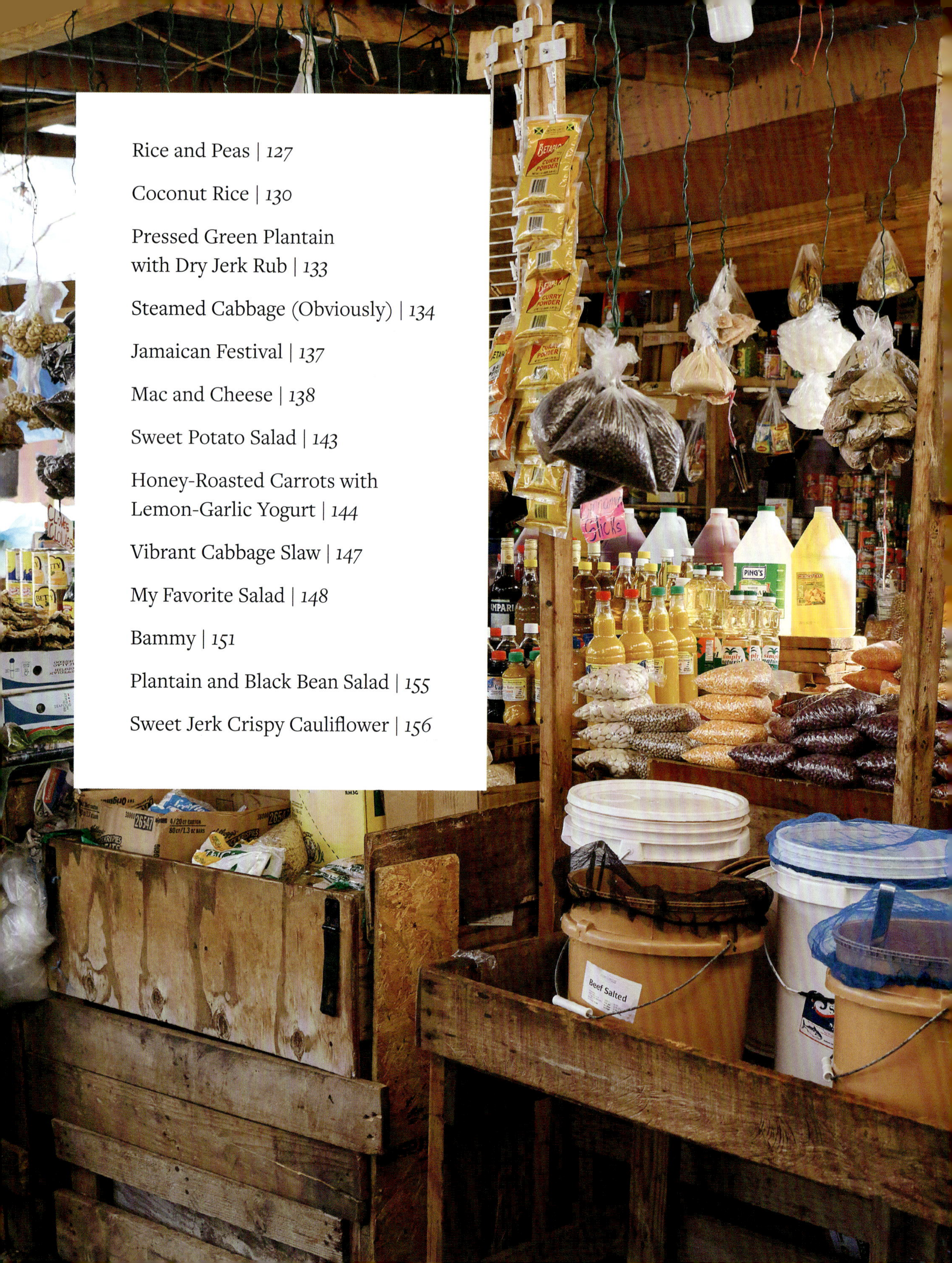
Beef Salted

A Jamaican celebration, whether of life or love, or a family dinner on Sunday, usually looks like this: laughter, raised voices (we're not quiet people), and plates heaped with food. Jamaicans love *food. And we don't believe in skimping, in either quantity or variety. So along with the main dish you will find at least three or four sides to go with it and to fill up all that empty space on your plate.*

Rice and Peas is both art and science, and no Jamaican feast is complete without it. Classics like Jamaican Festival are often served along with fried whole snapper and cold Red Stripe at seaside shacks. Pressed Green Plantain with Dry Jerk Rub is not at all traditional, but the combination of starch and heat is unbeatable. Innovative dishes like Sweet Jerk Crispy Cauliflower show you how Jamaican flavors can be incorporated into everyday meals in creative ways.

RICE AND PEAS

Serves 6

- 1 cup (225 g) dried red kidney beans (see Note)
- 1 small onion, diced
- 5 scallions, thinly sliced
- 5 thyme sprigs
- 4 garlic cloves, minced
- 1 Scotch bonnet pepper, left whole
- 1 tablespoon bouillon paste
- 2 teaspoons grated fresh ginger
- 2 teaspoons kosher salt, plus more to taste
- ½ teaspoon ground allspice
- One 14-ounce (400 ml) can coconut milk (1¾ cups)
- 2 tablespoons (1 ounce/30 g) butter
- 2½ cups (450 g) jasmine rice, rinsed

Rice and peas is arguably the most popular side dish in Jamaica. Nothing takes me home like the aroma of coconut-infused rice alongside the earthy scent of "peas" seasoned to perfection with the classic trio of thyme, scallion, and garlic. This dish pairs perfectly with mains like tender Curry Goat (page 170) and smoky Jerk Chicken (page 190).

Rinse the kidney beans, then place them in a large saucepan along with 6 cups (1½ L) water. Cover and let the beans soak for at least 5 hours or overnight.

Once the beans have soaked (do not drain), add the onion, scallions, thyme, garlic, Scotch bonnet, bouillon, ginger, salt, and allspice to the saucepan, place it over high heat, and bring to a boil. Reduce the heat to medium and simmer until the beans are tender, 30 to 45 minutes.

Add the coconut milk and butter and cook for another 10 minutes. Taste the liquid—you want it to be well seasoned because the rice will absorb it all, so add more salt if necessary.

Add the rice to the pot, stir gently (making sure not to break the Scotch bonnet), and reduce the heat to low. Cover and simmer, without stirring, until the rice is cooked through and all the liquid has been absorbed, 15 to 20 minutes.

Discard the Scotch bonnet and thyme stems and fluff the rice and peas with a fork. Serve hot.

NOTE: The beans need to soak for at least 5 hours, so plan ahead. To save time, you can substitute one 15.5-ounce (439 g) can kidney beans (liquid included) for the dried beans and reduce the amount of water in the recipe to 2 cups (500 ml).

VARIATION

Rice and Gungo Peas: Use dried or canned gungo peas (pigeon peas) in place of the kidney beans and follow the same instructions.

RICE AND PEAS AROUND THE WORLD

Depending on where you're from, you may know the dish as peas and rice, rice and peas, beans and rice, rice and beans, or even something else. Whatever you call it, these two belong together: Rice on its own and beans alone are not only boring but also incomplete proteins. Each lacks certain essential amino acids, but together, rice and beans contain all nine of the essential amino acids our body needs but can't produce on its own.

Both rice and beans have been around for a long, long time. Beans were recently carbon-dated to about ten thousand years ago in northeast Africa, and they have been cultivated and eaten in the Americas for about eight thousand years. Historians haven't been able to pinpoint exactly when or where rice was first farmed for food, but it's between four and seven thousand years ago somewhere in Asia. What we do know is that both rice and beans were introduced around the world by travelers of all kinds—explorers, pilgrims, soldiers, traders—who took the seeds with them on the road.

It's believed the ingredients ended up together in so many different places and in so many different ways for economic reasons. Beans and rice are both easy to grow and easy to store, and they are a valuable source of protein in places where animal sources are too expensive or just too hard to get. Dried beans are one of the cheapest sources of protein available, and because they're cheap, they've primarily been cooked and consumed by people with limited means. But we've done incredible things with the lowly bean.

In Louisiana, ham hocks and andouille sausage impart smoke, fat, and spice to rice and beans. Bahamian peas 'n rice uses dark brown pigeon peas, browning or burnt sugar, and tomato sauce. Their dish is also heavier, with salted pork and chunky vegetables added. Cubans make Moros y Cristianos—black beans cooked with white rice, spices, and bacon. Farther abroad, there is kitchari from India, a porridge-like mix of basmati rice and yellow mung beans simmered with cumin, turmeric, and ginger.

In Jamaica, our beloved rice and peas was traditionally made with pigeon peas, known locally as gungo peas. *Gungo* comes from an old English name for the Congo pea, thus named because of its cultivation around sub-Saharan Africa and use by those of African descent. At some point Jamaicans started using red beans instead of gungo peas because they were more widely available and often cheaper. The "peas" part of the name just stuck.

No matter which rice-and-bean dish you call your own, here's some bean math: 1 cup (185 g) dried beans = 2½ cups (480 g) cooked = two 15-ounce (425 g) cans.

COCONUT RICE

Serves 4

2 cups (340 g) jasmine rice, rinsed

One 14-ounce (400 ml) can coconut milk (1¾ cups)

2 teaspoons kosher salt

5 allspice berries

1 scallion, trimmed and cut in half

1 tablespoon (0.5 ounce/15 g) butter (see Note)

This savory coconut rice is a straightforward, easy-to-make side dish that can be ready in under 30 minutes. It is the perfect fusion of creamy coconut milk and fragrant jasmine rice, with subtle hints of allspice. It pairs well with stews like Oxtail and Butter Beans (page 163) or with Jerk Salmon with Herb Salsa (page 193). This recipe will be one you turn to again and again.

In a medium saucepan, combine the rice, coconut milk, 1 cup (250 ml) water, the salt, allspice berries, scallion, and butter. Give the ingredients a good stir. Place the saucepan over medium-high heat and bring to a boil.

Stir the rice again, reduce the heat to the lowest setting, cover the pot, and simmer until the rice is fully cooked, 15 to 20 minutes.

Discard the allspice berries and scallion. Fluff the rice with a fork. Serve hot.

NOTE: You can swap the butter out for olive oil if you want to keep this dairy-free.

RICE IS CULTURE

In 2021 Jamaicans consumed more than 200 million pounds (91,000 metric tons) of rice, according to the United Nations. That's roughly 88 pounds (40 kg) per person, more than three times as much as the average American, who consumed about 26 pounds (12 kg) of rice that year.

Rice has been a staple food for Caribbean people for generations. It's affordable and versatile and makes meals stretch. Rice became part of Caribbean diets through colonial trade routes, especially during the transatlantic slave trade, when foods that were cheap, filling, and easy to transport were needed to sustain enslaved people. Rice was also one of the foods, along with ingredients like yams and plantain, that was easy to grow in the tropical climate.

Over time, rice was adapted beautifully into the local cuisine. Its neutral taste allows it to absorb the bold, spiced flavors of Caribbean cooking, making it an ideal base for the region's famous dishes. For instance, Rice and Peas (page 127), cooked with coconut milk, thyme, and scallions, is a favorite pairing with Jerk Chicken (page 190) or Curry Goat (page 170). Rice, this way, isn't just a filler—it's a flavorful canvas that supports all the other ingredients.

Rice is also convenient. It can be stored for long periods, feeds a lot of people, and provides energy, which is important when physical labor is a feature of life. Rice works in all kinds of meals—as a side dish or a main paired with beans, fish, or vegetables. So, whether it's soaking up curry or making jerk chicken feel at home, rice is Jamaica's pantry powerhouse.

PRESSED GREEN PLANTAIN *with* DRY JERK RUB

Serves 4

Vegetable or other neutral oil, for deep-frying

2 green plantains

1 tablespoon Dry Jerk Rub (page 317) or store-bought jerk seasoning

1 lime, cut into wedges (optional)

You might think of these as tostones, but in Jamaica, we call them pressed green plantain (pronounced *plan-tin*). Whether you slice them into disks or on a bias, plucking them out of the hot oil at the right time during the first fry is critical. The second fry is complete when the plantain has reached your preferred level of doneness. Finish with a liberal sprinkle of dry jerk rub. These are best eaten fresh and hot from the pan.

Pour about 2 inches (5 cm) of oil into a medium heavy-bottomed saucepan and heat over medium heat to 350°F (177°C), or until the oil sizzles around a wooden spoon when it's dipped into the hot oil. Line a plate with paper towels and set it near the stove.

Peel each plantain by cutting the ends off, then making a slit in the skin along the length of the plantain with a sharp knife. Run your fingers along the inside of the skin to remove it completely and discard the peel. Slice each plantain into 8 pieces about 1 inch (2.5 cm) thick.

Working in batches, place the pieces of plantain into the hot oil and fry until golden and just tender, about 4 minutes. Remove the plantain from the oil using a slotted spoon and place on the paper towels to drain. Once they're cool enough to handle, gently press each plantain slice with the bottom of a glass or plate (see Note).

Return the pressed plantain to the hot oil in batches and fry until crispy and golden brown, another 2 minutes. Remove from the oil and place on the paper towels. Sprinkle with the jerk spice and serve with lime wedges, if desired.

NOTE: For crispier pressed plantain, press the slices as thin as they will go without breaking them. For plantain that is slightly chewier in the middle, press the slices to about ½ inch (1.5 cm) thick.

STEAMED CABBAGE (OBVIOUSLY)

Serves 4

3 tablespoons extra-virgin olive oil

4 ounces (115 g) Jamaican pumpkin (calabaza squash), peeled and cut into ¼-by-2-inch (1 cm by 5 cm) strips

1 medium onion, thinly sliced

1 medium carrot, cut into matchsticks

1 red bell pepper, sliced

3 garlic cloves, minced

Leaves from 2 thyme sprigs, chopped

¼ Scotch bonnet pepper, seeded and minced

¼ teaspoon ground allspice

½ large head green cabbage (about 1 pound/450 g), cored and thinly sliced

2 tablespoons (1 ounce/30 g) unsalted butter, cubed

1 teaspoon all-purpose seasoning, homemade (page 314) or store-bought

1½ teaspoons kosher salt

½ teaspoon freshly ground black pepper

This is a very uptown version of cabbage. We ate a lot of cabbage when I was growing up—it was an affordable and nutritious staple—but it wasn't like this! This recipe infuses tender green cabbage with fragrant thyme, fiery Scotch bonnet, and earthy allspice, transforming the mundane into something magnificent. Steamed cabbage goes perfectly with Brown Stew Chicken (page 178) and Fried Dumplings (page 79).

Heat the olive oil in a large skillet over medium heat. Add the pumpkin, onion, carrot, and bell pepper and cook until the onions are translucent and fragrant and the peppers have started to soften, about 5 minutes.

Add the garlic, thyme, Scotch bonnet, and allspice. Stir and continue to cook until the garlic and thyme are fragrant, about 2 minutes.

Add the cabbage, butter, 2 tablespoons water, the all-purpose seasoning, salt, and black pepper. Stir to combine, reduce the heat to medium-low, cover, and cook, stirring occasionally, until the cabbage has softened, 12 to 15 minutes. Taste and add more salt if necessary.

Serve immediately.

Store leftovers in an airtight container in the fridge for up to 3 days. Reheat on the stove or in the microwave.

JAMAICAN FESTIVAL

Makes 12

Vegetable oil or other neutral oil, for deep-frying

1½ cups (190 g) all-purpose flour

½ cup (80 g) fine yellow cornmeal

⅓ cup (70 g) sugar

2 teaspoons baking powder

1 teaspoon kosher salt

½ to ¾ cup (125 to 175 ml) whole milk or water

Cigar-shaped, deep-fried cornbread dough—Jamaican Festival is a party for your mouth. In Jamaica, a day at the beach isn't complete without a plate of fried fish and fresh-out-the-oil festival. The dough for this unique side is sweetened with a tups (little bit) of sugar. With just a handful of pantry staples, simple cornmeal dough is transformed into a crispy, savory bite that evokes memories of warm sand and cold beer.

Pour at least 2 inches (5 cm) of oil into a large saucepan and heat over medium heat to 325°F (165°C), or until the oil sizzles around a wooden spoon when it's dipped into the hot oil. Set a wire rack in a sheet pan or line a plate with paper towels and set it near the stove.

While the oil is heating, in a bowl, combine the flour, cornmeal, sugar, baking powder, and salt and stir to combine.

Add ½ cup (125 ml) of the milk to the flour mixture and stir until the dough just comes together. If it doesn't come together easily, add a little more milk, a tablespoon at a time, but not more than ¼ cup (60 ml). The dough should be smooth and soft but not sticky, and definitely not dry and crumbly. Use your hands to knead the dough for about 2 minutes, until it forms a smooth ball.

Divide the dough into 12 equal portions. Roll each portion with the palms of your hands into a cigar shape 3 to 4 inches (8 to 10 cm) long.

Working in batches to avoid overcrowding (the festival expand as they fry), add each piece of dough to the hot oil and fry until golden brown and cooked all the way through, 4 to 5 minutes, flipping them halfway through. Use a slotted spoon to transfer them to the wire rack or paper towels to drain. Serve immediately.

MAC AND CHEESE

Serves 8 to 10

1 pound (450 g) cavatappi or other spiral pasta

2 tablespoons kosher salt, plus more to taste

4 tablespoons (2 ounces/60 g) unsalted butter

1 small onion, diced

3 garlic cloves, minced

¼ teaspoon chile flakes (optional)

¼ cup (30 g) all-purpose flour

3 cups (750 ml) whole milk

1 teaspoon Dijon mustard

1 teaspoon Scotch Bonnet Sauce (page 310; optional)

1 teaspoon garlic powder

1 teaspoon onion powder

½ teaspoon smoked paprika

¼ teaspoon freshly grated nutmeg

1 cup (250 ml) heavy cream

3 cups (330 g) grated Gruyère cheese

3 cups (330 g) grated Monterey Jack cheese

2 cups (220 g) grated sharp yellow Cheddar cheese

½ cup (50 g) panko bread crumbs (optional)

My love affair with mac and cheese started at a young age, with the classic version from a box. Since then, I've had the Southern version, Trini mac pie, lobster mac and cheese, truffle mac and cheese, and too many others to count. You probably have your own go-to mac and cheese recipe, but this version is spiced up and full of flavor. You can use your favorite cheeses, but my preferences are Cheddar, Gruyère, and Jack. Bring it to your next family cookout, and I promise your friends and family will be coming back for seconds (or thirds).

Fill a pot with water and bring to a boil over high heat. Add the macaroni and salt and cook until the pasta is tender, according to the package directions. Drain the pasta and set aside.

Meanwhile, melt the butter in a pot over medium heat. Add the onion, garlic, and chile flakes (if using) and cook until the onions are translucent and fragrant, 2 to 3 minutes.

Reduce the heat to low and add the flour. Cook, stirring constantly, until the flour starts to smell a little nutty, 1 to 2 minutes. Pour in the milk in a slow stream while whisking to prevent lumps from forming, then scrape the bottom of the pan with a silicone spatula to ensure everything is incorporated.

Increase the heat to medium-low and bring the mixture to a simmer. Add the mustard, Scotch bonnet sauce (if using), garlic powder, onion powder, smoked paprika, and nutmeg. Cook, stirring occasionally, until the sauce thickens enough to coat a metal spoon, 4 to 5 minutes.

Add the cream, 2 cups (220 g) of the Gruyère, 2 cups (220 g) of the Monterey Jack, and the Cheddar and stir until the cheeses are melted. Pour the drained pasta into the pot. Stir to combine, taste the macaroni and cheese, and add more salt if needed.

recipe continues

Set a rack in the middle of your oven and heat the broiler to high. Spread the macaroni and cheese into a casserole dish. Top with the remaining 1 cup (110 g) Gruyère, the remaining 1 cup (110 g) Monterey Jack, and the panko (if using).

Broil on the middle rack of the oven until golden brown on top and bubbling, 3 to 6 minutes, rotating the pan if necessary so that it browns evenly. Let it cool for 10 minutes before serving.

Store leftovers in an airtight container in the fridge for up to 3 days.

SWEET POTATO SALAD

Serves 6

3 large red-skinned sweet potatoes (2 pounds/900 g total), peeled and cut into 1-inch (2.5 cm) cubes

1 tablespoon kosher salt, plus more to taste

1 cup (140 g) frozen green peas, thawed

¾ cup (170 g) mayonnaise

¼ cup (60 ml) red wine vinegar

1 red bell pepper, finely diced

½ red onion, finely diced

4 scallions, thinly sliced

½ bunch of flat-leaf parsley, chopped

2 tablespoons chopped fresh dill (optional)

2 garlic cloves, minced

1 tablespoon grainy mustard

1 tablespoon all-purpose seasoning, homemade (page 314) or store-bought

½ teaspoon freshly ground black pepper

½ teaspoon smoked paprika

The flesh of the sweet potato most commonly found in the Caribbean is firmer than that of the darker orange-fleshed sweet potatoes (often incorrectly called yams), making it perfect for potato salad. Red wine vinegar and grainy mustard bring in brightness, while the smoked paprika adds depth. This salad keeps well, so it's a great make-ahead dish.

In a large saucepan, combine the sweet potatoes and salt with enough water to cover. Bring to a boil over high heat, then reduce the heat to medium and cook until the potatoes are just tender but not soft or mushy, 10 to 15 minutes.

Drain the potatoes; transfer them to a large bowl and let cool slightly, about 15 minutes.

To the bowl, add the peas, mayonnaise, vinegar, bell pepper, red onion, scallions, parsley, dill, garlic, mustard, all-purpose seasoning, black pepper, and smoked paprika. Mix well to combine, then cover and refrigerate for at least 1 hour.

Once it has chilled, taste the sweet potato salad and add more salt if necessary. Serve chilled or at room temperature. Store leftovers in an airtight container in the fridge for up to 3 days.

HONEY-ROASTED CARROTS *with* LEMON-GARLIC YOGURT

Serves 6

For the yogurt

1 cup (215 g) whole-milk Greek yogurt

2 tablespoons honey

Grated zest of 1 lemon

1 tablespoon fresh lemon juice

1 garlic clove, minced

1 teaspoon kosher salt

For the carrots

2 pounds (900 g) carrots (about 10 large), peeled and halved lengthwise (see Note)

¼ cup (60 ml) honey, plus more for drizzling

2 tablespoons extra-virgin olive oil

Leaves from 3 thyme sprigs

2 teaspoons kosher salt

1 teaspoon grated fresh ginger

1 teaspoon ground cumin

½ teaspoon ground coriander

½ teaspoon ground turmeric

½ teaspoon smoked paprika

¼ teaspoon freshly ground black pepper

For garnish (optional)

Toasted sliced almonds

Mixed fresh herbs

This recipe uses common ingredients that are available everywhere. These honey-roasted carrots are simple to make, but the flavors are rich and complex. Lemon and garlic always taste great together, and in this recipe they show how changing up the way carrots are prepared can transform them from an everyday steamed or boiled side into something unexpectedly elegant. Serve alongside savory roasted meats like the Jerk Honey Butter Steak (page 229) or the Guinness-Braised Short Ribs (page 181).

Make the yogurt: In a small bowl, stir together the yogurt, honey, lemon zest, lemon juice, garlic, and salt. Let sit in the fridge until the carrots are ready to be served.

Make the carrots: Preheat the oven to 400°F (200°C).

In a large bowl, toss the carrots with the honey, olive oil, thyme, salt, ginger, cumin, coriander, turmeric, smoked paprika, and black pepper to evenly coat.

Arrange the carrots in a single layer on a large sheet pan, being careful not to overcrowd the pan. Use two sheet pans if you need to.

Roast until the carrots are tender and start to look slightly blistered in the oven, 30 to 40 minutes, stirring halfway through for even caramelization.

Remove the carrots from the oven and drizzle with another tablespoon or two of honey, then toss to coat. If desired, garnish with toasted almonds and fresh herbs. Serve immediately with the lemon-garlic yogurt.

NOTE: If your carrots are small (no more than 1 inch/2.5 cm in diameter), you can leave them whole once peeled. If they're jumbo carrots, quarter them lengthwise. If they're really long, cut them crosswise in half so you're left with pieces 4 to 5 inches (10 to 13 cm) in length.

VIBRANT CABBAGE SLAW

Serves 8

For the slaw

½ pineapple, peeled, cored, and sliced ¼ inch (6 mm) thick

1 poblano pepper, halved and seeded

½ large head green cabbage (about 1 pound/450 g), cored and thinly sliced

½ large head red cabbage (about 1 pound/450 g), cored and thinly sliced

1 large carrot, cut into thin matchsticks

1 red onion, thinly sliced

1 red bell pepper, thinly sliced

½ bunch of cilantro, chopped

Handful of fresh mint leaves

For the dressing

¼ cup (60 ml) red wine vinegar

¼ cup (60 ml) extra-virgin olive oil

2 tablespoons honey

Grated zest and juice of 1 lime

1 tablespoon grainy mustard

1 garlic clove, minced

1 teaspoon kosher salt

½ teaspoon freshly ground black pepper

¼ teaspoon ground cumin

Grilling the pineapple and poblano pepper to get just the right amount of caramelization is what makes this dish special. The char flavor adds depth and perfectly complements the freshness of the dressing and herbs here. This slaw tastes equally good at room temperature or chilled, so it's perfect for those busy days when you've got lots of other things going on and don't have time to fuss with food. Plus, the leftovers store well, making it a great option for meal prep.

Make the slaw: Heat an outdoor grill to high heat or preheat a grill pan on the stove over medium-high heat (see Note).

Grill the pineapple slices and the poblano halves until slightly charred on each side, about 3 minutes per side. Remove from the grill and let cool on a rack or baking sheet.

Cut the pineapple slices into thin strips. Peel the grilled poblano and cut it into thin slices about 1 inch (2.5 cm) long.

Transfer the grilled pineapple and grilled poblano to a large bowl. Add the green cabbage, red cabbage, carrot, red onion, bell pepper, and cilantro. Tear the mint leaves and add them to the bowl as well.

Make the dressing: In a small screw-top jar, combine the vinegar, oil, honey, lime zest, lime juice, mustard, garlic, salt, black pepper, and cumin. Give the jar a good shake to combine all the ingredients.

Pour the dressing over the cabbage slaw and toss with your hands or a pair of tongs until the slaw is fully coated and the cabbage has softened slightly. Serve at room temperature or chilled. Store leftovers in an airtight container in the fridge for up to 3 days.

NOTE: If your grill grates or grill pan aren't well seasoned or coated, spray with oil before heating so the pineapple doesn't stick. If you don't have a grill or a grill pan, you can cook the pineapple and poblano pepper in the oven for 20 minutes at 400°F (200°C).

MY FAVORITE SALAD

Serves 4 as a side or 2 as a main

For the dressing

½ cup (125 ml) extra-virgin olive oil

¼ cup (60 ml) red wine vinegar

2 tablespoons honey

1 teaspoon Dijon mustard

1 garlic clove, minced

Grated zest and juice of ½ orange

½ bunch of cilantro, roughly chopped

2 teaspoons kosher salt

½ teaspoon freshly ground black pepper

For the salad

1 bunch of kale, leaves stemmed and chopped or torn

Kosher salt and freshly ground black pepper

1 cup (180 g) cherry tomatoes, halved

1 avocado, cubed

¼ cup (40 g) toasted pumpkin seeds

4 ounces (115 g) soft goat cheese

Pickled Red Onions (recipe follows)

There are a lot of indulgent foods in Jamaican cuisine, but life is about balance, and this dish has just the right amount of everything. It has layers of texture and flavor thanks to the creamy avocado, tangy pickled onions, and crunchy toasted pumpkin seeds. The citrusy dressing is a harmonious mix of acidic, bright, and sweet and hits all the right notes. Serve the salad as a refreshing starter or a light side to complement heartier dishes like Honey-Ginger Chicken Thighs (page 196) or Coconut Steamed Red Snapper (page 182).

Make the dressing: In a blender, combine the olive oil, red wine vinegar, honey, mustard, garlic, orange zest, orange juice, cilantro, salt, and pepper and blend until smooth. (Alternatively, to make without a blender, see Note.) Store in an airtight container in the fridge until ready to use. The dressing will keep in the fridge for up to 1 week.

Make the salad: Place the kale in a bowl with 2 tablespoons of the dressing. Gently massage the dressing into the kale with your hands until the leaves become tender, about 1 minute. Taste the kale and season to taste with salt and pepper, if needed. Add the cherry tomatoes and avocado and toss gently so the avocado doesn't get mushy. Transfer to a serving bowl or to plates.

Top the salad with the pumpkin seeds, goat cheese, and some pickled red onions. Finish with another drizzle of the dressing and serve immediately.

NOTE: If you're making the dressing without a blender, finely chop the cilantro, then put all the dressing ingredients except the olive oil in a bowl. Whisk to combine and then slowly add the olive oil while whisking to create an emulsified dressing.

recipe continues

Pickled Red Onions

Makes about 2 cups (500 ml)

1 large red onion, thinly sliced

1 cup (250 ml) apple cider vinegar

2 tablespoons light brown sugar

1 tablespoon kosher salt

1 thyme sprig

Put the sliced red onions in a large jar or heatproof container.

In a small saucepan, combine ½ cup (125 ml) water, the apple cider vinegar, brown sugar, salt, and thyme. Bring to a boil over high heat and then pour the hot liquid over the sliced onions. Let cool completely, then store in the fridge until ready to use. (Pickled onions will keep in the fridge for up to 1 month.)

BAMMY

Makes 6

2 large cassavas (yucas; see Notes), peeled and cut into large chunks (about 2 pounds/900 g total)

2 teaspoons kosher salt

Vegetable oil or other neutral oil, for pan-frying

One 14-ounce (400 ml) can coconut milk (1¾ cups)

In Jamaica, you can buy bammy in any grocery store, or you can get it freshly made on the south coast. Few cooks make bammy at home; it's one of those things best bought, but this recipe challenges that norm. Whether you're up for the workout that is processing fresh cassava or you want to take the easier route with cassava flour (see Variation), you'll love this from-scratch version of a Jamaican staple. Bammy goes perfectly alongside Escovitch Whole Red Snapper (page 189) and is even better steamed and served with Coconut Steamed Red Snapper (page 182).

In a food processor, blend the cassava chunks until mostly smooth. Transfer the cassava to a cheesecloth and squeeze out the liquid to get it as dry as possible. If you don't have a cheesecloth, you can use a very fine-mesh sieve and try to get as much liquid out as possible. Transfer the drained cassava to a bowl and season with the salt.

Line a baking sheet with parchment paper. Scoop about 1 cup (190 g) of the cassava into a 4-inch (10 cm) ring mold (see Notes) and press the cassava into the mold to shape the bammy. Repeat until you have 6 uniform pieces. Place the formed bammy on the lined pan.

Heat a large skillet over low heat and add just enough oil to lightly coat the bottom of the pan, about 1 tablespoon. Working in batches so you don't crowd the pan, transfer the shaped bammy to the skillet and cook until lightly golden, about 8 minutes on each side, being careful when you flip them so they don't break apart. Transfer the fried bammy to a plate and repeat until all the bammy are cooked.

Pour the coconut milk into a wide, shallow bowl or pan. Add the bammy to the bowl and let them soak for about 10 minutes to absorb some of the coconut milk.

Set the same skillet over medium heat and add enough oil to lightly coat the bottom of the pan again. Fry each piece a second time until golden and crispy, about 2 minutes on each side. Serve immediately.

recipe continues

NOTES

- If you can't find fresh cassava, you can substitute frozen cassava, which usually comes pregrated or in large peeled chunks.
- If you don't have a ring mold, form the bammy by shaping 1 cup (190 g) of blended and drained cassava into a ball with your hands, then pressing down with a plate until it's about ½ inch (1 cm) thick.

VARIATION

Cassava Flour Bammy: In a large bowl, mix 3 cups (450 g) cassava flour and 2 teaspoons kosher salt. Add 1 cup (250 ml) water and incorporate well. If the dough doesn't come together immediately, add more water, a little at a time, until the mixture comes together as a stiff dough. The dough for the bammy should be firm. If it seems crumbly, add a little more water. If it seems too wet, add a little more cassava flour. Let the dough rest at room temperature, covered, for 30 minutes.

Cut the dough into 6 equal portions and shape each one into a ball. Dust a work surface with cassava flour. Roll each piece of dough with a rolling pin into a flat disk about ½ inch (1 cm) thick. Fry, soak, re-fry, and finish the bammy as directed.

CHOOSING THE BEST CASSAVA

You can find fresh cassava (also known as yuca or yuca root) at many large supermarkets, especially those with international food sections, as well as at Latin American, African, and Caribbean markets. When selecting fresh cassava, look for a bark-like brown skin and firm white or cream-colored flesh. Avoid roots with soft spots, deep cuts, bruises, or mold. Cassava should feel heavy for its size, indicating a high moisture content. Fresh cassava has a neutral smell, so avoid any with a sour or fermented odor.

Store fresh cassava in a cool, dry place for a few days, or refrigerate it wrapped in a paper towel inside a plastic bag for up to a week. For longer storage, peel, cut, blanch, and freeze the cassava. Before cooking, peel off the tough skin completely and trim off any woody parts.

PLANTAIN AND BLACK BEAN SALAD

Serves 6

2 ripe plantains, peeled and diced

¼ cup (60 ml) plus 2 tablespoons extra-virgin olive oil

1 teaspoon kosher salt, plus more to taste

1 teaspoon freshly ground black pepper

1 teaspoon smoked paprika

One 15-ounce (425 g) can black beans, drained and rinsed

1 red bell pepper, diced

½ large red onion, diced

½ bunch of cilantro, chopped

2 garlic cloves, minced

¼ cup (60 ml) apple cider vinegar

Grated zest and juice of 1 lime

1 tablespoon honey

½ teaspoon ground cumin

Jamaicans typically eat ripe plantain fried or boiled as a side dish. This salad offers a fresh alternative—roasting it, which intensifies the honey notes of the plantain. The black beans deliver a protein-packed creamy textural contrast. Even the pickiest of eaters will love this salad. The flavors intensify with time, making it a go-to for meal preppers, busy weeknights, or when you are bringing a dish to a party after a hectic work-week. Eat it on its own or as a topping for salad greens.

Preheat the oven to 400°F (200°C). Line a sheet pan with parchment paper.

In a bowl, toss the plantain with 2 tablespoons of the olive oil, the salt, ½ teaspoon of the pepper, and ½ teaspoon of the smoked paprika until coated. Spread the plantain evenly on the prepared pan.

Roast until tender and golden brown, about 15 minutes. Remove from the oven and let cool slightly.

In a large bowl, combine the black beans, bell pepper, red onion, cilantro, and garlic. Add the remaining ¼ cup (60 ml) olive oil, the vinegar, lime zest, lime juice, honey, cumin, and remaining ½ teaspoon pepper and ½ teaspoon smoked paprika. Stir to combine.

Once the plantain is cool enough to handle, add it to the bowl and stir everything until well combined. Season to taste with salt.

Serve immediately as a side dish or store in an airtight container in the fridge for up to 3 days; the salad is even better on the second day, once the flavors have had time to meld together.

SWEET JERK CRISPY CAULIFLOWER

Serves 2 to 4

Jerk isn't just for meat, and this crispy jerk cauliflower proves it. This recipe can be served as a vegetarian side or as part of a meat-free meal with Rice and Peas (page 127) and Steamed Cabbage (page 134).

For the honey jerk sauce

½ cup (125 ml) honey

¼ cup (60 ml) jerk marinade, homemade (page 315) or store-bought (see Note)

Grated zest and juice of 1 lime

1 tablespoon soy sauce

1 teaspoon grated fresh ginger

1 garlic clove, minced

For the cauliflower

Vegetable oil or other neutral oil, for deep-frying

½ cup (60 g) all-purpose flour

½ cup (65 g) cornstarch

1 tablespoon kosher salt

1 teaspoon garlic powder

1 teaspoon onion powder

1 teaspoon smoked paprika

¼ teaspoon freshly ground black pepper

1 cup (250 ml) cold club soda

1 small head cauliflower, cut into florets

For serving (optional)

Handful of cilantro, leaves torn

Handful of mint leaves, torn

3 scallions, thinly sliced on a bias

1 lime, cut into wedges

Make the jerk sauce: In a small saucepan, combine the honey, jerk marinade, lime zest, lime juice, soy sauce, ginger, and garlic. Bring to a boil over high heat, then reduce the heat to medium-low and cook until the sauce is syrupy, 3 to 5 minutes. Set aside until ready to use.

Fry the cauliflower: Pour about 3 inches (7.5 cm) of oil into a large heavy-bottomed saucepan and heat over medium-high heat to 375°F (190°C). Line a plate with paper towels and set it near the stove.

While the oil is heating, in a medium bowl, whisk together the flour, cornstarch, salt, garlic powder, onion powder, smoked paprika, and pepper. Add the club soda and whisk to make a smooth, runny batter, about the same consistency as crepe batter.

Working in batches so you don't overcrowd the pan, dip the cauliflower florets into the batter to coat them evenly, then drop them into the hot oil, working carefully so you don't burn yourself. Fry until golden brown and crispy, about 5 minutes. Transfer to the paper towels using a spider, slotted spoon, or tongs to drain. For extra-crispy cauliflower, fry the florets a second time for a few more minutes.

Once the cauliflower is all cooked, put it into a large bowl, pour in the sauce, and toss to coat. Serve immediately with cilantro, mint, scallions, and lime wedges, if desired.

This dish is best served freshly made, but leftovers will keep in an airtight container in the fridge for up to 2 days. To reheat, place the cauliflower in a 400°F (200°C) oven or air fryer until hot and crispy, 10 to 15 minutes.

NOTE: If you're using store-bought jerk marinade or paste, reduce the salt to 1 teaspoon since store-bought is saltier than homemade.

SIMMER DOWN

STEWS AND BRAISES

For Jamaicans, stews and braises are part of our history. Our ancestors depended largely on their enslavers for food, plus whatever they could grow on the provision ground, supplemented with wild food foraged or hunted nearby. They ate preserved meats, salted fish, dried beans. They ate yam and cassava, crabs and fish, and sometimes snakes. They added okra, callaloo, and hot peppers to enhance the flavor and nutritional value of their meals. And they cooked everything in one pot over a coal fire.

This chapter features traditional stews and braises like Brown Stew Chicken as well as my modern takes on a few—Guinness-Braised Short Ribs, for example. Most braises taste better the next day, and many require some advance preparation, like soaking beans or marinating meat, but they're so worth it.

OXTAIL AND BUTTER BEANS

Serves 6

3 pounds (1.4 kg) oxtail, cut into pieces at the joint (see Notes)

¼ cup (60 g) Jamaican green seasoning, homemade (page 308) or store-bought

4 tablespoons vegetable oil or other neutral oil

2 tablespoons all-purpose seasoning, homemade (page 314) or store-bought

2 teaspoons kosher salt, plus more to taste

1 teaspoon ground allspice

1 teaspoon freshly ground black pepper

1 teaspoon browning (optional; see Notes)

6 cups (1.5 L) beef stock (see Notes)

1 large onion, diced

1 Roma tomato, chopped

4 scallions, thinly sliced

6 garlic cloves, minced

Leaves from 4 thyme sprigs

1 Scotch bonnet pepper, left whole

1 tablespoon minced fresh ginger

2 bay leaves

1 teaspoon paprika

1 teaspoon garlic powder

1 teaspoon onion powder

ingredients continue

This dish marries tender, slow-cooked oxtail with creamy butter beans, creating a rich and flavorful meal perfect for any occasion. It makes the silkiest, most delicious gravy you will ever eat. A friend of mine once said, "Oxtail gravy is life," and he was right. And while Jamaica isn't the only culture that cooks oxtail, our treatment of it is as unapologetically unique as we are.

Place the oxtail in a large bowl along with the green seasoning, 2 tablespoons of the oil, the all-purpose seasoning, salt, allspice, pepper, and browning (if using). Mix with clean hands or a large spoon to coat the oxtail evenly. Marinate, covered, in the fridge for at least 1 hour, but preferably overnight.

Warm a Dutch oven or other large heavy pot over medium-high heat. Add the remaining 2 tablespoons oil and, working in batches, sear the oxtail until browned, 3 to 5 minutes on each side, and transfer to a plate or bowl.

Return all the seared oxtail to the pot. Add the beef stock, increase the heat to high, and bring the mixture to a boil. Reduce the heat to medium and cook the oxtail, covered, for 1 hour at a rapid simmer, stirring occasionally.

Add the onion, tomato, scallions, garlic, thyme, Scotch bonnet, ginger, bay leaves, paprika, garlic powder, onion powder, and 4 cups (1 L) water and stir. Reduce the heat to medium-low, cover the pot, and cook until the oxtail is tender and beginning to fall off the bones, another 2 hours, stirring every so often so the oxtail doesn't burn at the bottom of the pot.

Increase the heat to high and add the butter beans. Cook, uncovered, until the sauce has reduced slightly, another 20 minutes or so. Season to taste with salt. Discard the Scotch bonnet and bay leaves. Serve the stew hot with rice and peas.

recipe continues

One 15.5-ounce (439 g) can butter beans, drained and rinsed

Rice and Peas (page 127), for serving

Store leftovers in an airtight container in the fridge for up to 3 days (see Notes).

NOTES

- Most grocery stores and butchers sell oxtail precut, so don't worry about cutting it any further if it's already been jointed.
- The browning is optional, but it adds a richer color and some depth of flavor to the dish. You can find it in the international aisle of many grocery stores or at any Caribbean grocer.
- In place of the beef stock, you can use bouillon cubes dissolved in water.
- Don't be alarmed if the oxtail is a solid mass when you take leftovers out of the fridge—oxtail is quite gelatinous, so the gravy typically sets like Jell-O when it cools. It will loosen again once reheated.

OXTAIL EVOLUTION: PLANTATION SCRAPS TO PRIME CUTS

Enslaved Africans were given only the bare minimum of food. To make up for a lack of protein, they sought out cheap cuts of meat or the leftover bits of slaughtered animals that nobody else wanted. Wealthy plantation owners threw out the tails, hooves, offal, and other animal parts they deemed inedible, and my ancestors found creative ways to prepare and preserve them. They transformed oxtail—the tough tail end of a working beast—into a rich, soul-satisfying feast by slow braising, careful browning, and hours of low simmering, along with local herbs and spices.

Today, oxtail costs as much as a top sirloin steak. What you're getting at the supermarket these days are cross-cut sections of beef or veal tail, each a thick cylindrical piece of bone with chunks of meat and cartilage attached to it. Because of the high ratio of bone and cartilage to meat, oxtail needs to be cooked slowly over low heat for the best results. Prepared properly, this fatty, gelatinous mess gets melt-in-your-mouth-tender and is as delicious or even better than the best tenderloin.

STEW PEAS *with* PIG'S TAIL

Serves 6

2 cups (450 g) dried red kidney beans (see Notes)

2 pounds (900 g) cured pig's tail (see Notes), rinsed and cut into 2-inch (5 cm) chunks

1 pound (450 g) beef chuck, cut into 2-inch (5 cm) cubes

One 14-ounce (400 ml) can coconut milk (1¾ cups)

1 large onion, diced

4 scallions, sliced

6 garlic cloves, minced

Leaves from 4 thyme sprigs

1 Scotch bonnet pepper, left whole

1 tablespoon minced fresh ginger

1 teaspoon allspice berries

2 bay leaves

½ teaspoon freshly ground black pepper

Uncooked Spinners (page 106)

Cooked jasmine rice, for serving

Everything's better with bacon, but bacon is expensive, and pig's tail is the next best thing. The salty, fatty, addictive flavor holds a special place in Jamaican cuisine. In this hearty stew, pig's tail marries with tender red kidney beans (aka "peas") and rich beef chuck. The peas soak up the aromatic spices and creamy coconut milk to create a deeply satisfying stew. The addition of spinners brings an extra layer of texture to the dish. Just be sure to plan ahead, as this recipe requires soaking the peas and pig's tail for several hours before cooking.

Place the dried red kidney beans in a large bowl with 8 cups (2 L) water. Cover and soak for 5 to 8 hours at room temperature.

While the beans are soaking, place the pig's tail in another bowl and fill with enough water to cover. Place a lid or plastic wrap over the bowl and soak in the fridge for 5 to 8 hours.

Drain the pig's tail, transfer it to a large pot, and cover with fresh water. Bring to a boil over high heat and cook for 10 minutes.

Drain to remove the salty water, then fill the pot with enough fresh water to just cover the pig's tail. Add the cubed beef to the pot along with the soaked kidney beans and their soaking liquid. Bring to a boil over high heat, then reduce the heat to medium and cook until the beans and the meat are tender, 1 to 1½ hours.

Add the coconut milk, onion, scallions, garlic, thyme, Scotch bonnet, ginger, allspice, bay leaves, and black pepper. Increase the heat to medium-high and cook until the onions have softened and the liquid has reduced slightly, about 20 minutes.

Reduce the heat to medium-low and place the spinners into the pot one at a time. Cook until the dumplings are fully cooked and the sauce has thickened, 15 to 20 minutes.

recipe continues

Discard the bay leaves and allspice berries. Serve the stew and spinners immediately with jasmine rice. Store leftovers in an airtight container in the fridge for up to 3 days.

NOTES

- You can use three 15.5-ounce (439 g) cans of red kidney beans with their liquid instead of dried beans; just add them to the recipe after the pig's tail has been cooked. Note that this version will be a bit paler in color than if you use dried beans.

- Cured pig's tail can be found in many butcher shops, online, in the international section of many supermarkets, and in Caribbean supermarkets.

CURRY, BUT MAKE IT JAMAICAN

Curry, like many Jamaican foods, did not start its journey under happy circumstances. And despite what we've been led to believe, curry powder itself is not an ingredient in traditional Indian cooking. In fact, it was the British who invented it. During their colonization of India, the Brits developed a taste for the local cuisine. Wanting to bring the flavors back to England and to the colonies but with one repeatable, reliable flavor, they created curry powder. The basic curry powder typically contained coriander, cumin, turmeric, black pepper, ginger, and chile, all finely ground to be easily incorporated into various recipes. This curry powder made its way to Jamaica too.

After the abolition of slavery in 1834, a new system of indentured labor (which turned out to be not much better than slavery) began in the colonies. Between 1845 and 1917 about 37,000 Indian laborers made the journey to Jamaica. Separated by oceans from their families, their homes, and their culture, they embraced the closest thing to home they could find—the British version of their Indian flavors, curry powder.

They brought their techniques, added local seasonings, and gave us Curry Goat (page 170), roti (page 86), and tamarind.

Jamaican curry powders are a bit different from others. The main ingredient is turmeric instead of coriander (hence the signature bright yellow color), and they include some uniquely Caribbean spices like allspice, which adds a warm, woodsy note. Sometimes clove and fenugreek are added, but there is rarely a strong pepper component, since the heat is usually served up in the form of fresh Scotch bonnet peppers.

BETAPAC
CURRY POWDER
NET WT. 110 GRAMS (3.88 OZ.)
MANUFACTURED IN JAMAICA BY
BETAPAC LIMITED
BETAPAC
BLACK PEPPER
NET WT. 110 GRAMS (3.88 OZ.)
Cinnamo
Sticks

CURRY CHICKEN

Serves 4

2 pounds (900 g) boneless, skinless chicken thighs, cut into 2-inch (5 cm) cubes

1 medium yellow onion, diced

4 tablespoons vegetable oil, other neutral oil, or extra-virgin olive oil

3 tablespoons Jamaican curry powder

3 garlic cloves, minced

1 tablespoon minced fresh ginger

2 teaspoons kosher salt, plus more to taste

½ teaspoon freshly ground black pepper

¼ teaspoon ground allspice

½ Scotch bonnet pepper, seeded and minced

2 cups (500 ml) chicken stock

4 scallions, thinly sliced

Leaves from 4 thyme sprigs

1 large Yukon Gold potato, cut into 1-inch (2½ cm) cubes

1 large carrot, diced

Mango Chutney (page 318), for serving

Roti (page 86), for serving (optional)

The Jamaican way of preparing curry chicken is unique: We marinate the meat with all the seasonings, including the curry powder. And before the seasoned chicken goes into the pot, we "burn" the curry—that is, we cook curry powder in hot oil to bring out the aroma, flavor, and color. To intensify the flavors even more, the meat is then seared in this hot curry oil before the other ingredients are added. The end result is tender, incredibly flavorful chicken that pairs perfectly with the sweet tang of mango chutney and roti to soak up the gravy.

In a large bowl, combine the chicken, onion, 2 tablespoons of the oil, 2 tablespoons of the curry powder, the garlic, ginger, salt, black pepper, allspice, and Scotch bonnet. Mix with clean hands or a large spoon to coat the chicken evenly with the seasonings. Marinate, covered, in the fridge for at least 30 minutes and preferably overnight.

Heat the remaining 2 tablespoons oil in a large pot over medium heat. Add the remaining 1 tablespoon curry powder and cook, stirring constantly, until fragrant and slightly browned, 30 seconds to 1 minute. Add the marinated chicken and stir to coat with the browned curry powder. Cover the pot and cook for 10 minutes, stirring occasionally.

Increase the heat to medium-high and add the chicken stock, scallions, thyme, potato, and carrot. Cook, uncovered, until the potatoes are tender and the sauce has thickened, 15 to 20 minutes.

Season to taste with more salt, if needed. Serve immediately with mango chutney and roti, if desired.

Store leftovers in an airtight container in the fridge for up to 3 days.

CURRY GOAT

Serves 6

3 pounds (1.4 kg) goat stew meat (see headnote)

½ cup (120 g) Jamaican green seasoning, homemade (page 308) or store-bought

4 tablespoons vegetable oil, other neutral oil, or extra-virgin olive oil

3 tablespoons Jamaican curry powder

2 tablespoons all-purpose seasoning, homemade (page 314) or store-bought

1 tablespoon kosher salt, plus more to taste

1 teaspoon freshly ground black pepper

1 teaspoon ground allspice

1 large yellow onion, diced

6 garlic cloves, minced

4 scallions, thinly sliced

Leaves from 4 thyme sprigs

1 Scotch bonnet pepper, left whole

1 tablespoon minced fresh ginger

1 teaspoon allspice berries

1 teaspoon garlic powder

1 teaspoon onion powder

2 large Yukon Gold potatoes, cut into 1-inch (2.5 cm) pieces

Coconut Rice (page 130), for serving

Mango Chutney (page 318), for serving

You'll want to find a good butcher to procure the goat meat for this recipe. Meat from older animals tends to be tough and can take hours of cooking to break down. Unfortunately, most goat meat is kept in the freezer section, so there's no way to know what you're getting. If the meat is still tough after the prescribed cooking time, pour yourself another Rum and Coco (page 291), settle down, and let it simmer. It can take as long as two and a half hours to become tender, but however long it takes, curry goat is worth the wait.

In a large bowl, combine the goat meat, green seasoning, 2 tablespoons of the oil, 2 tablespoons of the curry powder, the all-purpose seasoning, salt, black pepper, and ground allspice. Cover and marinate in the fridge for at least 1 hour and preferably overnight.

Heat the remaining 2 tablespoons oil in a large pot over medium heat. Add the remaining 1 tablespoon curry powder. Cook, stirring constantly, until fragrant and slightly browned, 30 seconds to 1 minute. Add the marinated goat and stir to coat with the browned curry powder. Cover the pot and cook for 10 minutes, stirring occasionally.

Add enough water to cover the goat meat by about 2 inches (5 cm) and stir. Increase the heat to medium-high, cover, and cook for 1 hour.

Reduce the heat to medium. Add the yellow onion, garlic, scallions, thyme, Scotch bonnet, ginger, allspice berries, garlic powder, and onion powder and cook, uncovered, until the goat is tender, another 45 minutes to 1 hour. If the liquid reduces too much, add a little more water so that the goat stays partially submerged.

Add the potatoes and cook until they are tender, about 20 minutes.

Season to taste with salt. Discard the Scotch bonnet and allspice berries. Serve immediately with coconut rice and chutney.

Store leftovers in an airtight container in the fridge for up to 3 days; this dish is even better the next day.

COCONUT CURRY LOBSTER

Serves 4

4 shell-on lobster tails (1½ to 2 pounds/680 to 900 g total)

3 tablespoons extra-virgin olive oil

4 teaspoons Jamaican curry powder

2 teaspoons all-purpose seasoning, homemade (page 314) or store-bought

4 tablespoons coconut oil

1 medium onion, chopped

8 scallions, 3 chopped and 5 cut into 3-inch (7.5 cm) pieces

½ Scotch bonnet pepper, seeded and chopped

Leaves from 2 thyme sprigs

½ teaspoon ground turmeric

¼ teaspoon ground allspice

2 cups (500 ml) vegetable stock

One 14-ounce (400 ml) can coconut milk (1¾ cups)

1 small potato, about 4 ounces (115 g), cut into chunks

1 small carrot, chopped

1 bay leaf

1 teaspoon kosher salt, plus more to taste

ingredients continue

Coconut curry lobster offers a different way to highlight the range of flavor that is possible with curry. The secret lies in cooking and blending the vegetables, herbs, and spices into a silky, creamy sauce before the lobster is added. This technique preserves the integrity of the delicate lobster meat and avoids the risk of overcooking it. Enjoy this dish immediately for the best texture and flavor, though leftovers can be gently reheated.

Using a sharp knife or a pair of kitchen scissors, cut each lobster tail in half lengthwise, then cut each half into 3 or 4 pieces, about 2 inches (5 cm) each, keeping the shell on. Rinse the cut lobster meat under cold water to remove any shell fragments and place in a bowl big enough to fit all the lobster. Gently toss the lobster with the olive oil, 2 teaspoons of the curry powder, and the all-purpose seasoning. Set aside.

Heat 2 tablespoons of the coconut oil in a medium saucepan over medium-high heat. Add the onion, chopped scallions, Scotch bonnet, and thyme and cook until the onions are fragrant and slightly translucent, about 3 minutes. Add the remaining 2 teaspoons curry powder, the turmeric, and the allspice and cook for another minute, stirring constantly, until the spices are fragrant.

Stir in the vegetable stock, coconut milk, potato, carrot, bay leaf, and salt. Increase the heat to medium-high and bring to a boil, then reduce the heat to medium-low and simmer until the potatoes and carrots are cooked through, 15 to 20 minutes.

While the sauce is cooking, heat the remaining 2 tablespoons coconut oil in a large sauté pan over high heat. Add the seasoned lobster meat and cook until the lobster starts to turn bright orange, about 3 minutes. Transfer the lobster to a large bowl and set aside, keeping the empty pan on the stove.

recipe continues

For serving

Handful of cilantro, for garnish

1 lime, cut into wedges

Coconut Rice (page 130)

Mango Chutney (page 318)

Once the potatoes and carrots are tender, discard the bay leaf and transfer the sauce with the potatoes and carrots, to a blender. Blend until smooth. (You may need to work in batches if you have a smaller blender.)

In the same pan you used for the lobster, cook the 3-inch (7.5 cm) pieces of scallion over high heat until they start to soften and lightly brown, about 2 minutes. Return the lobster to the pan, pour in the blended curry sauce, and reduce the heat to medium. Cook, stirring frequently, until the lobster is fully cooked, another 3 to 5 minutes. Season to taste with salt.

To serve: Garnish with a handful of cilantro and lime wedges for squeezing and serve with the rice and chutney. This lobster is best when eaten immediately, but leftovers can be reheated over the stove or in the microwave—note that the lobster may not be as tender when you reheat it.

ALMOST ITAL CURRY VEGETABLE STEW

Serves 4

3 tablespoons coconut oil

1 large onion, diced

4 garlic cloves, thinly sliced

Leaves from 3 thyme sprigs

1 tablespoon minced fresh ginger

½ Scotch bonnet pepper, seeded and minced

1 tablespoon Jamaican curry powder

1 teaspoon ground turmeric

½ teaspoon ground cumin

½ teaspoon ground coriander

8 ounces (225 g) Jamaican pumpkin (calabaza squash), peeled and diced

1 large red bell pepper, diced

1 cup (250 ml) vegetable stock

One 15.5-ounce (439 g) can chickpeas, drained and rinsed

One 14-ounce (400 ml) can coconut milk (1¾ cups)

1 teaspoon kosher salt, plus more to taste

¼ teaspoon freshly ground black pepper

Coconut Rice (page 130), for serving

2 scallions, thinly sliced on a bias, for garnish

Chopped fresh cilantro, for garnish

This curried vegetable stew is a nod to Ital cuisine. It's a quick and easy dish that's perfect for busy weeknights or when you want a hearty, flavorful meal without the fuss (or the meat). This recipe combines pumpkin, bell pepper, and chickpeas with rich coconut milk and aromatic spices, delivering a satisfying stew with great depth of flavor. Feel free to add any other veggies you have on hand, or even tofu. Garnish with fresh scallions and cilantro and serve it over coconut rice for a simple and beautiful meal in under 30 minutes.

Heat the coconut oil in a pot over medium heat. Add the onion, garlic, thyme, ginger, and Scotch bonnet and cook, stirring occasionally, until the onions are translucent, 4 to 5 minutes.

Add the curry powder, turmeric, cumin, and coriander and cook, stirring frequently, until fragrant, 1 to 2 minutes.

Increase the heat to medium-high, add the pumpkin and bell pepper, and cook until the vegetables are evenly coated with the spices, about 2 minutes.

Add the vegetable stock, chickpeas, coconut milk, salt, and black pepper. Bring to a boil, then reduce the heat to medium-low and simmer, stirring occasionally, until the pumpkin is tender and the stew has thickened slightly, 15 to 20 minutes. Season to taste with more salt, if desired.

Serve immediately with coconut rice, garnishing with the scallions and cilantro before serving.

ITAL IS VITAL

The first Ital meal I ever ate was cooked by a Rasta named Bravo. People thought he was my grandfather. His skin was light, like mine, and the lines in his face and the gray in his dreadlocks told the story of a hard life. Bravo was one of Mama Cherry's many Rasta friends who congregated in a yard in downtown Kingston. They gathered to smoke the chalice, chant, and drum while a big pot of Ital stew bubbled over a coal fire. You had to be a Rasta or close friends with one to be allowed in this yard, and Mama Cherry was almost both.

Being a true Rasta is about living a pure and natural lifestyle to increase livity, or life energy. The Ital—from the word *vital*—way of eating emphasizes fresh fruits, vegetables, legumes, and whole grains, aligning with the principle of living close to the earth. There aren't any meats, salt, sugar, oils, or artificial or man-made ingredients in the diet. There are therefore no trans fats and only healthy fats. Ital dishes are also cooked in a way that preserves their nutrients, so most foods are steamed, stewed, or grilled, and rarely fried. This approach to cooking is rooted in the belief that natural foods enhance life energy and spiritual vitality and serve as a way to honor the body as a temple of Jah.

Ital eating is not just for health but also for the spirit. Rastas believe you are what you eat and that what you put into your body affects your mind and soul. It is a way of living in harmony with nature and respecting all living things. Which is why most Rastas avoid meat, especially pork, believing it to be unclean.

I always say Mama Cherry was almost a Rasta because she wore her hair in dreadlocks and enjoyed her ganja and her positive vibes, but she could never be a true Rasta because she loved jerk pork too much.

Many Rastas prefer to eat from a calabash, a gourd that grows naturally in Jamaica. It symbolizes a return to natural, earth-friendly practices and reinforces the Rastafari values of self-reliance, respect for the earth, and use of natural materials.

Ital cuisine is more relevant than ever today. As people become more aware of how diet affects health and the environment, the principles of Ital eating offer a great model for sustainable and healthy living. I do enjoy a little Ital cooking now and then, but I'm not quite ready to give up my jerk pork!

BROWN STEW CHICKEN

Serves 6

3 pounds (1.4 kg) bone-in chicken drumsticks and thighs (separated at the joint), skin removed

1 medium onion, diced

6 garlic cloves, minced

4 scallions, sliced

4 tablespoons vegetable oil, other neutral oil, or extra-virgin olive oil

2 tablespoons all-purpose seasoning, homemade (page 314) or store-bought

1 tablespoon kosher salt, plus more to taste

1 tablespoon minced fresh ginger

2 teaspoons browning

1 teaspoon smoked paprika

½ teaspoon ground allspice

½ teaspoon freshly ground black pepper

2 cups (500 ml) chicken stock

1 large carrot, cut into 1-inch (2.5 cm) pieces

1 medium green bell pepper, thinly sliced

1 Roma tomato, chopped

1 Scotch bonnet pepper, left whole

Leaves from 4 thyme sprigs

2 bay leaves

Jamaican brown stew chicken is known for its rich, savory, and slightly sweet flavor profile, which sets it apart from other chicken dishes. Marinating ensures the spices have a chance to really permeate the chicken. The traditional way of making this dish is to caramelize sugar, but browning takes less time and makes this recipe foolproof. Though this version is a shortcut from the traditional preparation, it still delivers all the flavor.

Place the chicken in a large bowl along with the onion, garlic, scallions, 2 tablespoons of the oil, the all-purpose seasoning, salt, ginger, 1 teaspoon of the browning, the smoked paprika, allspice, and black pepper. Toss to coat the chicken well, cover, and marinate in the fridge for at least 30 minutes and ideally overnight.

Heat the remaining 2 tablespoons oil in a large saucepan over medium-high heat. Working in batches, remove the chicken from the onion and seasoning mixture and sear until golden, about 2 minutes on each side. Remove from the pan and set aside.

Reduce the heat to medium. Add the onion and seasoning mixture to the pan and cook until fragrant, about 3 minutes. Return the chicken to the pan and add the stock, the remaining 1 teaspoon browning, the carrot, bell pepper, tomato, Scotch bonnet, thyme, and bay leaves. Increase the heat to medium-high, cover, and cook for 20 minutes.

Uncover the pot and continue to cook, stirring occasionally, until the chicken has cooked through, the carrots are tender, and the sauce has reduced by half, another 15 minutes.

Season to taste with salt. Discard the bay leaves and Scotch bonnet. Serve the stew immediately.

Store leftovers in an airtight container in the fridge for up to 3 days.

GUINNESS-BRAISED SHORT RIBS

Serves 6 to 8

3 to 4 pounds (1.4 to 1.8 kg) boneless beef short ribs, cut into 3- to 4-inch (8 to 10 cm) pieces

3 tablespoons kosher salt, plus more to taste

4 tablespoons extra-virgin olive oil

2 tablespoons smoked paprika

2 tablespoons garlic powder

1 tablespoon freshly ground black pepper

½ teaspoon cayenne pepper

2 carrots, diced

2 celery stalks, diced

1 large yellow onion, diced

6 garlic cloves, smashed

Leaves from 4 thyme sprigs

2 cups (500 ml) beef stock

One 14.5-ounce (411 g) can diced tomatoes

1 bottle (375 ml) Guinness stout or other dark stout (1½ cups)

¼ cup packed (55 g) dark brown sugar

¼ cup (60 ml) Worcestershire sauce

3 bay leaves

Guinness stout has been in Jamaica for a long time—at least since the early 1800s—and was originally shipped there to satisfy the desires of Irish workers on the island. In the 1970s, Jamaican brewing company Desnoes & Geddes began to bottle and distribute Guinness Extra Foreign Stout under contract, guaranteeing both freshness and the character expected of a Guinness stout. It remains a favorite brew for many Jamaicans, partly because we believe that anything bitter is good for you, partly because the high alcohol content gives good bang for the buck, and partly because it's so good in Guinness Punch (page 298)—and these braised short ribs.

In a large bowl, combine the beef, salt, 2 tablespoons of the olive oil, the smoked paprika, garlic powder, black pepper, and cayenne and mix with your hands until the beef is thoroughly coated. Cover and marinate for at least 30 minutes and ideally overnight.

Warm a large heavy-bottomed pot or Dutch oven over medium-high heat. Pour the remaining 2 tablespoons oil into the pot and, working in batches, sear the beef on all sides until browned, about 3 minutes on each side. Remove from the pot and set aside on a plate.

Reduce the heat to medium. Add the carrots, celery, onion, garlic, and thyme to the pot and cook, stirring frequently, until the onion is translucent and fragrant, about 4 minutes.

Add the beef stock, diced tomatoes, Guinness, brown sugar, Worcestershire sauce, and bay leaves and stir, scraping the bottom of the pot with a heatproof spatula. Bring to a simmer, then add the short ribs back to the pot and stir. Reduce the heat to medium-low and cook until the meat is tender, 2 to 2½ hours.

Discard the bay leaves and serve the short ribs immediately.

Store leftovers in an airtight container in the fridge for up to 3 days.

COCONUT STEAMED RED SNAPPER

Serves 4

4 red snapper fillets, skin on or off (about 6 ounces/170 g each)

1 tablespoon all-purpose seasoning, homemade (page 314) or store-bought

2 tablespoons coconut oil

1 small onion, thinly sliced

1 medium carrot, cut into thin strips

3 garlic cloves, thinly sliced

½ Scotch bonnet pepper, seeds removed and sliced

Leaves from 2 thyme sprigs

1 teaspoon allspice berries

One 14-ounce (400 ml) can coconut milk (1¾ cups)

8 okra pods, cut on a bias into 1-inch (2.5 cm) pieces

1 red bell pepper, thinly sliced

1 teaspoon kosher salt

½ teaspoon freshly ground black pepper

4 tablespoons (2 ounces/60 g) cold salted butter, cubed

2 scallions, thinly sliced on a bias, for garnish

Bammy (page 151), for serving (optional; see Note)

Every Jamaican has a favorite version of steamed fish. Some love it in a spicy broth, others prefer just the head in a curry-laced gravy, and still others, like me, enjoy it this way: snapper fillets poached in coconut milk with lots of allspice berries and Scotch bonnet pepper. The okra will make the sauce a bit viscous, so if you don't like that texture, leave out the okra. For me, though, the mucilage—which is the scientific but unfortunate term for the okra slime—gives the sauce a beautiful silky texture that's enhanced by the nuanced flavors of this versatile seedpod.

Sprinkle the snapper fillets with the all-purpose seasoning and set aside.

Heat the coconut oil in a large skillet over medium-high heat. Add the onion, carrot, garlic, Scotch bonnet, thyme, and allspice and cook, stirring constantly, until the onions have softened, about 3 minutes.

Add the coconut milk, okra, bell pepper, salt, and black pepper and bring to a boil over high heat. Reduce the heat to medium and cook until the vegetables have softened, about 5 minutes.

Gently place the fish in the pan and spoon some of the sauce over the fillets. Place a tablespoon of the butter on top of each piece of fish, cover the pan, and cook until the fish is cooked through, 10 to 15 minutes.

Discard the allspice berries. Serve immediately in a shallow bowl. Ladle the sauce and vegetables over the fish and garnish with the scallions. If desired, serve with bammy.

NOTE: If serving with bammy, poach the bammy in the sauce for 15 minutes before adding the fish to the pan. If your pan is big enough, you can cut the bammy and arrange them in the pan alongside the fish.

THE OLD *and* THE NEW

FAVORITE DISHES REIMAGINED

Jamaicans have a strong sense of tradition, and we cling with incredible tenacity to the way things have always been done. With food, this means respecting old ways and hanging on to recipes passed down through generations. These dishes remind us where we come from and connect us to our roots.

Some recipes—like Escovitch Whole Red Snapper—are best eaten the way they always have been, but I also like to play with traditional flavors and present them in unique and surprising ways. Some of my favorite dishes, like the Jerk Smash Burger with Bacon Jam and Coffee-Cocoa Lamb Chops, mix the old with the new. These recipes show how Jamaican food can stay true to its roots while being fresh and exciting. They also capture a taste of home, something Jamaicans living abroad crave on the daily.

ESCOVITCH WHOLE RED SNAPPER

Serves 2

Vegetable oil or other neutral oil, for deep-frying

2 whole red snappers (1 pound/450 g each), scaled and gutted

2 tablespoons all-purpose seasoning, homemade (page 314) or store-bought

1 teaspoon kosher salt

½ teaspoon freshly ground black pepper

¼ teaspoon ground allspice

1 cup Escovitch Pickle (page 309)

Escovitch snapper is one of those traditional recipes that's perfect as is. For this dish, start with a good-quality whole snapper; frying it whole and bone-in keeps the fish juicy and intact. Once you've fished it out of the hot oil and doused it with the spicy escovitch pickle, it's best to dig into the whole snapper immediately. Just be careful navigating around the bones.

Pour about 2 inches (5 cm) of oil into a pot that's large enough to fit both pieces of fish. Heat over medium-high heat to 350°F (177°C), or until the oil sizzles around a wooden spoon when it's dipped in the hot oil. Line a plate with paper towels and set it near the stove.

While the oil is heating, make 3 slits ½ inch (1 cm) deep along each side of the fish. Combine the all-purpose seasoning, salt, pepper, and allspice in a small bowl and season the inside and outside of the fish with this mix.

Once the oil is hot, place each snapper into the oil and fry until fully cooked and crispy, about 5 minutes on each side. Place the fried snapper on the paper towels to drain.

Serve immediately with a generous amount of escovitch pickle on top. This dish is best served fresh and hot.

Store leftovers in an airtight container in the fridge for a day or two. Reheat in an air fryer or oven at 375°F (190°C) for 10 to 15 minutes.

VARIATION

Substitute whole red snappers with 2 whole lobsters or lobster tails, sliced down the middle lengthwise. Season the meat side of the lobster halves (no need to score the meat), then follow the recipe as written, reducing the cooking time to 5 minutes, or until the meat is opaque and cooked through.

JERK CHICKEN OUTDOORS OR IN THE OVEN

Serves 4

1 whole chicken (3 to 4 pounds/1.4 to 1.8 kg), backbone removed (see Notes)

½ cup (125 ml) jerk marinade, homemade (page 315) or store-bought (see Notes)

2 tablespoons all-purpose seasoning, homemade (page 314) or store-bought

1 tablespoon Jamaican green seasoning, homemade (page 308) or store-bought

1 tablespoon kosher salt

2 cups applewood chips, if grilling (optional)

Making Jamaican jerk is a little bit art and a little bit science, and real jerk is best left to the pros. The traditional method demands that the meat be slow-cooked and smoked over a charcoal fire and infused with the smoke of pimento wood. But most of us don't have access to pimento wood or even a smoker, so this is neither possible nor practical. This recipe is the next best thing to that roadside jerk pit taste.

The secret is in the marinade—a perfect blend of garlic, thyme, scallions, and Scotch bonnet peppers balanced with the sweetness of molasses. Marinating the chicken overnight maximizes the flavor, after which you can roast it in the oven or fire up the grill for some slow-cooked perfection. Baked or grilled, the result is a mouthwatering masterpiece.

Use a sharp knife to make incisions along the legs, thighs, and breasts of the chicken. Pat the chicken dry with a paper towel and place it in a large bowl or zip-seal bag.

Add the jerk marinade, all-purpose seasoning, green seasoning, and salt to the chicken. Rub the seasonings into the chicken, making sure to get the marinade under the skin as well. Marinate the chicken in the fridge overnight or for at least 2 hours.

To cook the chicken in the oven: Preheat the oven to 425°F (220°C). Line a sheet pan with parchment paper.

Lay the chicken flat, skin-side up, on the lined pan and pour any excess marinade onto the chicken. Roast the chicken until nicely browned, 45 minutes to 1 hour, spooning some of the juices over the chicken twice during this time. You should have a few charred bits on the skin when it's done, and the juices from the chicken should run clear when you cut into the meat. You can also check the chicken with a meat thermometer; it should read 165°F (74°C).

recipe continues

Let cool slightly, then cut the chicken into pieces and serve immediately.

To cook the chicken on the grill: Preheat a grill to 450°F (230°C). Wrap the wood chips, if using, in foil, poke a few holes in the top and bottom of the foil pack with a knife, and place it on the grill.

Once the wood chips start to smoke, place the chicken on the grill, skin-side up, and close the grill. Lower the heat to around 250° to 300°F (120° to 150°C) and cook the chicken, with the grill closed, for about 1½ hours, flipping it halfway through, until the surface is nicely browned, with some charred bits on the skin, and a meat thermometer inserted into the thickest part of the thigh reads 165°F (74°C). Serve immediately.

NOTES

- You can ask your butcher to remove the backbone of the chicken or use a pair of sharp kitchen shears to cut it out yourself. This will allow the chicken to cook faster and more evenly.
- If you're using store-bought jerk marinade or paste, reduce the salt to 1 or 2 teaspoons since store-bought is saltier than homemade.

JERK SALMON *with* HERB SALSA

Serves 4

- 4 salmon fillets (4 ounces/115 g each), about 1 inch (2.5 cm) thick, skin removed
- ¼ cup (30 g) Dry Jerk Rub (page 317) or store-bought jerk seasoning
- 4 tablespoons extra-virgin olive oil
- Herb Salsa (recipe follows), for serving
- 1 lime, cut into wedges, for serving

Here is a light and fresh interpretation of jerk. Salmon is marinated with robust seasonings and pan-seared to perfection. The zesty herb salsa combines the freshness of cilantro, the heat of Scotch bonnet, and the tang of lime. If you're not feeling herby, try the Mango Salsa (page 217) with this salmon instead. This recipe is perfect for everyday dinners and special occasions alike and embodies the bold, dynamic spirit of Jamaican cuisine. Enjoy it with a squeeze of lime to bring all the flavors together.

Season the salmon generously with the jerk seasoning and 2 tablespoons of the olive oil, making sure to get both sides of the fish fully coated with spices.

Heat a large cast-iron skillet over medium-high heat. Pour the remaining 2 tablespoons oil into the pan. As soon as the oil starts to smoke lightly, add the fish, skin-side up, and cook until browned nicely, 3 to 4 minutes.

Gently flip each piece with a fish spatula. Reduce the heat to medium and cook on the other side until the fish is fully cooked, another 3 to 4 minutes. Remove from the heat and lift the fish onto a plate.

Spoon some of the herb salsa on top of the fish and serve with a wedge of lime.

recipe continues

Herb Salsa

Makes ½ cup **(*110 g*)**

3 tablespoons extra-virgin olive oil

2 tablespoons honey

2 tablespoons apple cider vinegar

2 scallions, thinly sliced

1 garlic clove, minced

Grated zest and juice of 1 lime

1 teaspoon kosher salt

½ teaspoon minced fresh ginger

½ bunch of cilantro, finely chopped (stems included)

¼ Scotch bonnet pepper, seeded and minced

¼ teaspoon ground cumin

In a bowl, combine the olive oil, honey, vinegar, scallions, garlic, lime zest, lime juice, salt, ginger, cilantro, Scotch bonnet, and cumin. Mix well and set aside until ready to serve. (The herb salsa can be made up to 1 day ahead, covered, and stored in the fridge.)

HONEY-GINGER CHICKEN THIGHS

Serves 4

2 pounds (900 g) boneless, skinless chicken thighs

¼ cup (30 g) cornstarch

1 teaspoon kosher salt

1 teaspoon garlic powder

1 teaspoon onion powder

2 tablespoons vegetable oil or other neutral oil

½ cup (125 ml) soy sauce

3 tablespoons honey

3 tablespoons light brown sugar

2 tablespoons minced fresh ginger

1 tablespoon toasted sesame oil

½ teaspoon chile flakes

4 garlic cloves, thinly sliced

4 scallions, cut into 3-inch (7.5 cm) pieces

Coconut Rice (page 130), for serving (optional)

Asian flavors are among my favorite. This recipe pays homage to the Chinese influence on Jamaican cuisine, a legacy of the Chinese immigrants who arrived on the island between 1890 and the 1940s. The chicken dish combines sweet and savory flavors and pairs perfectly with coconut rice.

Pat the chicken thighs dry with paper towels, then place them in a bowl and add the cornstarch, salt, garlic powder, and onion powder. Toss to coat.

Heat the vegetable oil in a large skillet over medium-high heat. Working in batches to avoid overcrowding, add the chicken thighs and cook the chicken until golden brown and slightly crispy, 4 to 6 minutes on each side.

While the chicken is cooking, in a small bowl, stir together ¼ cup (60 ml) water, the soy sauce, honey, brown sugar, ginger, sesame oil, chile flakes, garlic, and scallions.

Once the chicken is golden on each side, remove it from the pan and set aside. Add the sauce to the same pan and cook until bubbling, 2 to 3 minutes.

Return the chicken to the pan and coat with the sauce. Cook over medium heat, stirring the sauce so it doesn't burn, for another 2 minutes on each side.

Serve immediately with coconut rice, if desired.

FROM PIT TO PLATE: THE JERK STORY

There is jerk pork, jerk chicken, or jerk lobster if you're fancy. But what is jerk, besides the perfect mix of spicy, smoky, and fragrant? It's an important part of Jamaica's history, for starters.

About 1,400 years ago the Taino people migrated from South America to Jamaica, forming communities all over the island. According to historical records, the Taino were not only Jamaica's first people but also the world's first pit masters. To cook and preserve meats, including fish and wild game, they would dig a pit and make a slow fire in it, cover the fire with a grate of green wood lashed together with fibers, then put meat on the wood frame above the fire and let it cook slowly. They called this process *barabicu*, which meant "sacred pit."

Several hundred years later, the Maroons (Africans who had escaped their British enslavers and fled to the mountains) had settled among the remaining Tainos, most of whom had been wiped out by Spanish colonization by that time. The Maroons tweaked the barabicu method: Meats were heavily seasoned and marinated using ingredients like bird peppers and pimento—both of which were plentiful and native to the island—and thyme. This combination was crucial for both flavor and preservation. The meat was wrapped in leaves and placed on pimento wood over a low fire in a pit covered with branches and leaves to hide the smoke from the colonizers. The new method also kept the meat moist, leaving it tender and succulent. This process of slow-cooking and smoking heavily seasoned meat is central to what we now know as jerk.

Jerk eventually made its way from the mountains to the beach and is now arguably the most popular street food on the island and a staple of Jamaican cuisine. Modern versions use grills, ovens, or even stovetops, adapting to contemporary cooking methods.

As native pimento trees and bird peppers became more difficult to find, the jerk recipe was also adapted: Sweetwood and wild coffee wood are now used to flavor the meat in some jerk centers, and Scotch bonnet peppers have replaced bird peppers. Over time, other seasonings have been added too—garlic, onion, scallion, ginger—but if it doesn't have hot peppers, allspice, and thyme, it's not jerk.

Jerk seasoning is now available in jars or bags on supermarket shelves around the world. It has influenced the modern culinary scene across the globe, from jerk chicken wraps in Alaska to jerk fried tofu in Japan. I like to sneak the fragrant heat of jerk seasoning into unexpected places, like Jerk Street Corn (page 55) and my favorite burger of all time, the Jerk Smash Burger (page 211).

GRILLED LOBSTER *with* SCOTCH BONNET GARLIC BUTTER

Serves 4

Kosher salt

4 large lobster tails (6 to 8 ounces/170 to 225 g each), preferably from Caribbean spiny or Atlantic lobsters

8 ounces (225 g) salted butter, at room temperature

8 garlic cloves, minced

1 lime, zested and then cut into wedges for serving

¼ cup (about 10 g) chopped fresh chives

¼ cup (15 g) chopped fresh parsley

½ Scotch bonnet pepper, seeded and minced

Whether you're using fresh or frozen, Atlantic or spiny, parboiling lobster before grilling it ensures plump, perfectly cooked meat that separates easily from the shell. The combination of lime zest, white-hot grill heat, and butter infused with garlic and Scotch bonnet elevates this dish, evoking the flavors of that first unforgettable time you had it on your Jamaican getaway.

Fill a large pot with water and add a generous handful of salt—it should taste like the ocean. Bring the salted water to a boil over high heat. While the water comes to a boil, prepare an ice bath for the lobster by filling a large bowl, or another large pot, with ice and enough cold water to cover.

Once the water is boiling, add the lobster tails and cook them for 2 to 3 minutes or until the meat is just starting to turn opaque. Transfer the parcooked lobster tails to the ice bath to cool completely, then take the tails out of the ice bath and cut them in half lengthwise with a sharp knife. Arrange the tail halves cut-side up on a sheet pan and set aside.

Heat a grill (see Note) to 450°F (230°C).

While the grill heats, in a small bowl, combine the butter, garlic, lime zest, chives, parsley, and Scotch bonnet. Season to taste with salt, then smother each lobster tail half with about 2 tablespoons of the butter mixture.

When the grill is hot, place the lobster tails on the grill, cut-side up. Cook for 3 minutes, then flip the pieces and cook until lightly charred, about 2 minutes. Remove from the heat and serve immediately with the lime wedges.

NOTE: If you don't have a grill, use a stovetop grill pan or your oven's broiler set to high. If you're using the broiler, don't flip the lobster tails.

MAMA CHERRY'S FRIED CHICKEN... ALMOST

Serves 6

2 cups (500 ml) whole milk

2 tablespoons distilled white vinegar

3 to 4 pounds (1.4 to 1.8 kg) bone-in, skin-on chicken drumsticks and thighs, separated at the joint

2 tablespoons kosher salt

1 tablespoon onion powder

1 tablespoon garlic powder

1 teaspoon smoked paprika

1 teaspoon dried thyme

1 teaspoon dried oregano

1 teaspoon freshly ground black pepper

1 teaspoon chili powder or cayenne pepper

For the dredge

3 cups (375 g) all-purpose flour

1½ tablespoons kosher salt

1 tablespoon onion powder

1 tablespoon garlic powder

1 teaspoon smoked paprika

2 teaspoons freshly ground black pepper

1 teaspoon chili powder or cayenne pepper

Vegetable oil or other neutral oil, for deep-frying

Honey Jerk Sauce (page 156), for serving (optional)

Mama Cherry never wrote out the recipe for her amazing fried chicken (or anything else, for that matter). But I do remember how she'd wash a whole chicken with lime juice and white cane vinegar, cut it into pieces, and season it with the same ingredients she would later use in the flour dredge. And she always added a Scotch bonnet pepper and a few allspice berries to the hot oil to season it.

This recipe takes the best parts of Mama Cherry's fried chicken and elevates it. Here the seasoned buttermilk bath is the secret weapon. If you have time, let the chicken marinate in it overnight; the acid in the buttermilk tenderizes the meat and adds a subtle tang. Serve with honey jerk sauce for a little sweet heat alongside this mouthwatering dish.

In a large bowl, stir together the milk and vinegar and let rest until the milk begins to curdle slightly, 5 to 10 minutes (this is homemade buttermilk!).

Add the chicken, salt, onion powder, garlic powder, smoked paprika, thyme, oregano, black pepper, and chili powder to the buttermilk. Use your hands or a pair of tongs to massage the spices and buttermilk into the chicken. Cover the bowl and let it sit in the fridge for at least 1 hour, or overnight if possible, to marinate.

Make the dredge: About 20 minutes before you're ready to cook the chicken, in a large bowl, mix together the flour, salt, onion powder, garlic powder, smoked paprika, black pepper, and chili powder. Set aside.

Pour about 4 inches (7.5 cm) of oil into a large pot and heat over medium heat to 325°F (163°C), or until the oil sizzles around a wooden spoon when it's dipped in the hot oil.

recipe continues

While the oil is heating, dredge the chicken with the flour mixture (see Note). Working in batches, fry each piece until golden brown and fully cooked, flipping halfway through, 12 to 15 minutes.

Serve immediately with honey jerk sauce, if desired.

NOTE: To dredge the chicken, working one piece at a time, remove the chicken from the buttermilk marinade and place in the flour mixture. Use your hands to press some of the flour mixture into the chicken pieces, making sure all sides of the chicken are evenly coated. Shake off any excess flour, then rest the chicken pieces on a wire rack or a sheet pan. Let the dredged chicken sit for 10 to 15 minutes before frying.

VARIATION

Extra-Crunchy Fried Chicken: Coat the chicken pieces in the flour mixture as instructed, then drizzle a little of the buttermilk marinade on top of the chicken. Press more of the flour mixture into the chicken, shake off any excess, and fry as described above.

JERK BBQ PORK RIBS

Serves 6 to 8

For the pork ribs

2 racks St. Louis–style pork ribs (2½ to 3 pounds/1.1 to 1.4 kg each)

½ cup (125 ml) jerk marinade, homemade (page 315) or store-bought (see Note)

¼ cup (60 ml) extra-virgin olive oil

2 tablespoons kosher salt

1 tablespoon smoked paprika

2 teaspoons garlic powder

2 teaspoons onion powder

1 teaspoon dried thyme

1 teaspoon ground allspice

1 teaspoon freshly ground black pepper

1 teaspoon chili powder

2 large yellow onions, sliced into 1-inch-thick rings

For the jerk BBQ sauce

1 cup (250 ml) ketchup

½ cup (110 g) packed dark brown sugar

¼ cup (60 ml) apple cider vinegar

¼ cup (60 ml) jerk marinade, homemade (page 315) or store-bought (see Note)

½ cup (125 ml) freshly squeezed orange juice

ingredients continue

A lot of rib recipes intimidate home cooks with the need to poach or steam and grill or broil. Not this one. Here the ribs are baked in a super-easy method. The controlled temperature of baking and the use of St. Louis–style spareribs (thicker, breast-bone-off pork ribs) ensures juicy meat that falls off the bone.

Prepare the pork ribs: Place the ribs on a sheet pan. In a small bowl, combine the jerk marinade, olive oil, salt, smoked paprika, garlic powder, onion powder, thyme, allspice, black pepper, and chili powder. Generously season both sides of the ribs with the spice rub. Cover the ribs and marinate in the fridge for at least 2 hours or up to 24 hours.

When you're ready to cook the ribs, preheat the oven to 350°F (180°C).

Line a roasting pan with foil and arrange the onion slices evenly on the tray. Pour about 2 cups (500 ml) water into the roasting pan. Place the ribs over the onions and cover the roasting pan tightly with foil. Bake until the ribs are tender, 1½ to 2 hours.

Meanwhile, make the jerk BBQ sauce: In a small saucepan, combine the ketchup, brown sugar, vinegar, jerk marinade, orange juice, Worcestershire sauce, garlic powder, onion powder, smoked paprika, black pepper, and salt to taste. Cook over low heat, stirring frequently, until slightly thickened, about 10 minutes.

Once the ribs are tender, carefully remove the foil covering the ribs and brush a generous amount of the BBQ sauce on the ribs with a pastry brush or basting brush. Increase the oven temperature to 450°F (230°C) or to a low broil and cook the ribs until they develop a nice char, another 5 to 10 minutes, brushing the ribs with BBQ sauce two more times during this time.

Let the ribs rest for 5 minutes before slicing and serving.

recipe continues

NORDICWARE®
INTERNATIONAL

- 1 tablespoon Worcestershire sauce
- 1 teaspoon garlic powder
- 1 teaspoon onion powder
- 1 teaspoon smoked paprika
- ½ teaspoon freshly ground black pepper
- Kosher salt

Store leftovers in an airtight container in the fridge for up to 3 days. To reheat, wrap the ribs in foil and heat them in a 300°F (150°C) oven for 20 minutes or until fully reheated.

NOTE: If you're using store-bought jerk marinade, reduce the amount of jerk marinade in the spice rub to ¼ cup (60 ml) and to 2 tablespoons in the BBQ sauce, since store-bought jerk is usually stronger than homemade jerk marinade.

BUT WHY "JERK"?

There are several theories about where the term "jerk" came from. One says it's from the Spanish *charqui*, while another says it refers to how the meat is turned or "jerked" around on the grill to ensure even cooking. A third relates to the method of cooking, where holes are "jerked" or poked into the meat to allow the marinade to penetrate. We may never know the full story, but coincidentally—or not—*jook* (which sounds a lot like jerk) is the Jamaican word for "poke."

CRISPY JERK PORK BELLY

Serves 3 or 4

2 to 3 pounds (900 g to 1.4 kg) pork belly, skin on

¼ cup (60 ml) jerk marinade, homemade (page 315) or store-bought

Kosher salt

1 teaspoon smoked paprika

1 teaspoon garlic powder

1 teaspoon onion powder

½ teaspoon freshly ground black pepper

2 tablespoons vegetable oil or other neutral oil

Mango Chutney (page 318), for serving (optional)

I like to think of myself as the king of crispy pork belly. It's a self-appointed title, to be sure, but try this recipe and tell me if you disagree. Marinated with a bold jerk seasoning and cooked to perfection, this pork belly has crunchy, crackling skin and succulent, flavorful meat. The key is in the preparation: poking the skin, scoring the meat, and allowing it to dry out for that signature crackle. A final blast in the oven transforms the skin into a golden, crispy delight. Serve it with a mango chutney for a hint of sweetness that perfectly balances the savory, spicy flavors.

Pat the skin side of the pork belly dry with a clean towel or paper towel. Using an ice pick, sharp knife, or meat tenderizer tool, poke as many holes in the skin of the pork belly as you can. Make sure to poke holes across the entire skin, but avoid going any deeper than the skin. (Alternatively, you can score lines across the pork skin, about ½ inch/1 cm apart, with a sharp knife.) Flip the pork belly and score cuts ½ inch (1 cm) deep lengthwise on the meat side of the pork belly, then turn the pork belly 90 degrees and score more cuts in the meat to create a crosshatched pattern.

In a small bowl, mix together the jerk marinade, 1 tablespoon salt, the smoked paprika, garlic powder, onion powder, and pepper. Rub the mix into the meat side of the pork belly until fully coated.

Transfer the pork belly to a container or sheet pan, skin-side up, and rub the skin of the pork belly with 2 tablespoons salt, then refrigerate, uncovered, for at least 4 hours or up to 24 hours (overnight is ideal) to allow the skin to dry out.

Preheat the oven to 375°F (190°C).

recipe continues

Pat the pork skin dry with a paper towel again, then rub the oil onto the skin and sprinkle with some more salt. Transfer the pork belly to a sheet pan, skin-side down, and top it with a piece of parchment paper. Place a heavy cast-iron pan or other heavy ovenproof dish on top of the pork belly to weight it down. This will help the skin cook evenly.

Cook the pork belly for 1 hour. Remove the cast-iron pan and parchment paper. Increase the oven heat to 400°F (200°C). Gently flip the pork belly over and cook skin-side up until the skin has puffed up and is crispy, another 15 to 20 minutes.

Let the pork rest for 10 minutes, then slice and serve with mango chutney if desired.

Store leftovers in an airtight container in the fridge for up to 3 days. Reheat in the oven, in a skillet, or in the air fryer, or use them to make Jerk Pork Chow Mein (page 219).

JERK SMASH BURGER *with* BACON JAM

Serves 4

- 1 pound (450 g) ground beef, 80% lean
- 1 tablespoon jerk marinade, homemade (page 315) or store-bought
- 2 teaspoons kosher salt
- 1 teaspoon garlic powder
- 1 teaspoon onion powder
- 1 teaspoon smoked paprika
- ½ teaspoon freshly ground black pepper
- Vegetable oil or other neutral oil, for frying
- 4 to 8 slices American cheese (see Note)
- ¼ cup (70 g) Bacon Jam (recipe follows)
- 4 potato buns or other soft burger buns
- 12 pickle slices
- Jerk Mayo (page 319)
- Butter lettuce (optional), for serving

These smash burgers are f*cking delicious. They're a bold twist on a classic favorite, merging Jamaican heat with the irresistible charm of American burgers. Each bite bursts with layers of flavor—juicy beef patties infused with jerk seasoning and topped with melted American cheese. But the real star here is the rich, sweet, and smoky bacon jam, balancing perfectly with the heat from the jerk mayo. Serve them on soft potato buns with pickles and crisp lettuce for a burger experience that's as satisfying as it is unforgettable.

In a large bowl, combine the beef, jerk marinade, salt, garlic powder, onion powder, smoked paprika, and pepper. Mix with your hands until well combined, then divide the mixture into 8 portions. Roll each portion into a ball.

Warm a large skillet over high heat. Add about 2 tablespoons of oil to the pan. Working in batches of 1 to 2 burgers (depending on the size of your pan), place balls of beef in the pan. Working quickly, place a square of parchment on top of the beef and press it flat with a weighted grill press or a heavy saucepan, until the beef starts to brown and develop a crispy edge, about 30 seconds. Remove the press and the parchment paper, then flip the patty and cook the other side for another 1 to 2 minutes.

Cover each patty with a slice of American cheese and cook until melted. Repeat this process until you've cooked all the burgers.

To assemble the burgers, spread a tablespoon of bacon jam on the bottom of each bun, then top with 3 pickle slices, 2 burger patties, a tablespoon of jerk mayo, and some lettuce (if using). Add the top of each bun and serve immediately.

recipe continues

Store leftovers, unassembled, in separate airtight containers in the fridge for up to 2 days. To reheat, put the patties in the microwave or reheat on the stove before assembling.

NOTE: This recipe makes double burgers—if you want only 1 slice of cheese on your burger, then put cheese on only 4 of the 8 patties when cooking.

Bacon Jam

Makes about 2 cups (545 g)

1 pound (450 g) thick-cut smoked bacon, cut into ½-inch (1 cm) strips

1 small yellow onion, diced

3 garlic cloves, minced

1 Roma tomato, diced

½ red bell pepper, diced

1 teaspoon minced fresh ginger

1 teaspoon fresh thyme leaves

1 cup (220 g) packed light brown sugar

½ cup (125 ml) apple cider vinegar

½ cup (125 ml) brewed coffee

Kosher salt

Line a plate with paper towels and set it near the stove. Cook the bacon in a cast-iron skillet over medium heat, stirring frequently, until it is lightly browned and most of the fat has rendered out, 8 to 10 minutes. Transfer the bacon with a slotted spoon to the paper towels to drain.

Add the onions to the same skillet and cook until translucent, about 3 minutes. Add the garlic, tomato, bell pepper, ginger, and thyme and cook until softened slightly, another 3 minutes.

Add the brown sugar, vinegar, and coffee and bring to a simmer. Reduce the heat to low, return the bacon to the pan, and cook until the mixture is syrupy, about 15 minutes, stirring occasionally. Season to taste with salt.

Cool and store in an airtight container in the fridge for up to 2 weeks.

ESCOVITCH FISH SANDWICHES

Serves 6

For the fried cod

Vegetable oil or other neutral oil, for deep-frying

1½ pounds (680 g) cod fillets (see Notes)

2 teaspoons kosher salt

1 teaspoon garlic powder

1 teaspoon onion powder

½ teaspoon freshly ground black pepper

½ teaspoon smoked paprika

¾ cup (90 g) all-purpose flour

¼ cup (30 g) cornstarch

1 teaspoon baking powder

1 cup (250 ml) cold Red Stripe beer (see Notes)

For the sandwiches

6 Coco Breads (page 76), for serving (see Notes)

Scotch Bonnet Mayo (page 319)

Escovitch Pickle (page 309)

Handful of cilantro

Lime wedges (optional), for squeezing

When I developed this recipe for Miss Lily's Negril, I took inspiration from the fish and chips you find all over England, but I wanted it to have a distinctly island flavor. Enter Scotch bonnet mayo and escovitch pickle. It's a simple and delicious way to taste the Caribbean.

Make the fried cod: Pour about 2 inches (5 cm) of oil into a large saucepan and heat over medium heat to 350°F (177°C). Line a sheet pan or wire rack with paper towels and set it near the stove.

While the oil is heating, cut the fish into strips about 4 by 2 inches (10 by 5 cm). Season with 1 teaspoon of the salt and the garlic powder, onion powder, black pepper, and smoked paprika. Set aside.

In a bowl, combine the flour, cornstarch, baking powder, and remaining 1 teaspoon salt and whisk until combined. Add the beer and mix until a smooth batter forms. The batter should resemble a light crêpe batter; if it's too thick, add more beer.

Working in batches to avoid overcrowding, dip each piece of seasoned fish in the batter. Let any excess batter drip off the fish and then carefully place it into the hot oil. Cook the fish until golden brown and fully cooked, 2 to 3 minutes on each side. Using a slotted spoon, transfer the fish to the lined pan or rack to drain.

Assemble the sandwiches: Open each coco bread and spread a generous amount of Scotch bonnet mayo on the inside of the bread. Top the bread with a couple of pieces of fried fish, some escovitch pickle, and cilantro. Serve immediately with a wedge of lime, if desired. It's best to eat these when they're fresh, as leftovers won't keep well.

NOTES

- Cod, snapper, tilapia, and grouper will all work in this fish sandwich.
- You can use any lager in this recipe or substitute cold club soda.
- You can substitute store-bought burger buns, such as a soft brioche bun, in place of the coco breads for this recipe.

GRILLED SWORDFISH *with* MANGO SALSA

Serves 2

Two 4- to 6- ounce (115 to 170 g), 1-inch-thick (2.5 cm) swordfish steaks

2 tablespoons extra-virgin olive oil

2 garlic cloves, minced

Grated zest and juice of 1 lime

2 teaspoons kosher salt

½ teaspoon chile flakes

½ teaspoon smoked paprika

½ teaspoon freshly ground black pepper

Mango Salsa (recipe follows)

Swordfish is one of the best fish for grilling—its firm, meaty texture holds together on the grill and its mild taste works well with both subtle and bold flavors. If you can't find swordfish, you can substitute halibut, mahi-mahi, or tuna. You can also use Herb Salsa (page 195) instead of the mango salsa as a topper, if you wish. And if you don't have a grill you can use a grill pan on your stove or the broiler in your oven. This dish is equally perfect for an outdoor summer barbecue or for a winter's dinner for two.

Place the swordfish steaks in a shallow tray and top with the olive oil, garlic, lime zest, lime juice, salt, chile flakes, smoked paprika, and black pepper. Rub the seasoning into the fish and set aside for 15 minutes to marinate while you make the mango salsa.

Heat an outdoor grill or a stovetop grill pan to medium-high heat (make sure you oil the grill or grill pan if it isn't nonstick). Add the swordfish steaks and cook until they are lightly charred and the flesh is opaque, 4 to 6 minutes on each side. Remove from the heat and let rest for 5 minutes.

Spoon the mango salsa over the fish and serve immediately.

Mango Salsa

Makes 2 cups

3 tablespoons extra-virgin olive oil

1 tablespoon red wine vinegar

1 garlic clove, minced

1 large ripe mango, diced

1 small avocado, diced

1 small shallot, diced

Grated zest and juice of 1 lime

½ jalapeño pepper, seeded and minced

½ red bell pepper, diced

Handful of fresh cilantro, chopped

Salt and freshly ground black pepper

In a large bowl, combine the olive oil, vinegar, garlic, mango, avocado, shallot, lime zest, lime juice, jalapeño, bell pepper, and cilantro and mix until combined. Season to taste with salt and pepper and store in the fridge until ready to serve with the fish.

CURRY CRAB FRIED RICE

Serves 4 to 6

¼ cup (60 ml) vegetable oil or other neutral oil

1 small onion, minced

4 scallions, white parts only, thinly sliced

8 garlic cloves, minced

2 tablespoons minced fresh ginger

½ Scotch bonnet pepper, seeded and minced

1 tablespoon Jamaican curry powder

4 cups (630 g) day-old cooked jasmine rice (see Note)

1 pound (450 g) jumbo lump crabmeat

½ cup (80 g) frozen green peas, thawed

2 tablespoons soy sauce

1 tablespoon toasted sesame oil

½ teaspoon ground white pepper (optional)

1 tablespoon toasted sesame seeds, for serving

½ bunch of cilantro, leaves torn, for serving

For this dish you can use precooked crabmeat or any other cooked protein of your choice. Shrimp, lobster, chicken, pork, or beef will all work well. You can also use leftover Coconut Rice (page 130), but whatever rice you choose, it should be cooked ahead of time and left overnight (or at least for a few hours) to dry out. This extra step helps ensure your fried rice isn't mushy.

Heat a wok, large skillet, or Dutch oven over medium heat. Add the vegetable oil, onion, and scallion whites and cook, stirring constantly, until fragrant and softened slightly, 3 to 4 minutes.

Increase the heat to medium-high. Add the garlic, ginger, Scotch bonnet, and curry powder and cook until the curry powder starts to brown slightly and the mixture is fragrant, 1 to 2 minutes.

Add the cooked rice and stir until it is fully coated with the curry, breaking up any clumps of rice. Cook until the rice is hot and starting to brown slightly, 4 to 5 minutes.

Add the crabmeat, green peas, soy sauce, sesame oil, and white pepper (if using) and stir gently so the crabmeat doesn't break up too much. Cook until the crab is hot, another 3 to 5 minutes.

Serve immediately with a sprinkle of sesame seeds and torn cilantro leaves.

NOTE: If you didn't make and dry out your rice ahead of time, cook the rice, spread it on a sheet pan, and freeze it for a couple of hours instead. You'll need to let the rice thaw before cooking, but this will help it dry out.

JERK PORK CHOW MEIN

Serves 6

One 12-ounce (340 g) package chow mein noodles (see Notes)

¼ cup (60 ml) chicken stock or water

¼ cup (60 ml) soy sauce (see Notes)

3 tablespoons hoisin sauce

3 tablespoons mirin

1 tablespoon jerk marinade, homemade (page 315) or store-bought

1 tablespoon rice vinegar

1 tablespoon cornstarch

1 tablespoon sugar

1 teaspoon toasted sesame oil

3 tablespoons vegetable oil or other neutral oil

6 scallions, cut into 2-inch (5 cm) pieces, plus more for garnish

6 garlic cloves, minced

2 tablespoons minced fresh ginger

½ Scotch bonnet pepper, seeded and minced

½ to 1 pound (225 to 450 g) leftover Crispy Jerk Pork Belly (page 208), leftover Jerk Chicken (page 190), or any other protein you prefer, sliced

3 heads baby bok choy, chopped

1 large carrot, cut into thin strips 3 inches (7.5 cm) long

½ small head green cabbage, thinly sliced

Two things I love about this recipe: It's great for using up leftovers and it's a perfect quick dinner or weekend lunch. This dish brings together the bold, spicy flavors of Jamaica with the savory, umami-rich notes of Chinese cuisine. Leftover crispy jerk pork belly is the heavy hitter in this chow mein. The Scotch bonnet pepper adds a kick that plays perfectly off the smoky jerk seasoning, while the mirin and sesame oil give a subtle nod to traditional Asian flavors.

Cook the noodles according to the package directions. Rinse with cold water and set aside.

In a small bowl, whisk together the stock, soy sauce, hoisin sauce, mirin, jerk marinade, rice vinegar, cornstarch, sugar, and sesame oil. Set aside.

Heat the vegetable oil in a large wok or skillet over high heat. Add the scallions, garlic, ginger, and Scotch bonnet and cook, stirring constantly, until the garlic and ginger begin to brown slightly, about 1 minute. Add the sliced pork belly and cook for another 2 minutes.

Add the bok choy, carrot, and cabbage and cook until the vegetables start to soften slightly, 2 to 3 minutes. Add the cooked noodles and the sauce to the wok and stir until the sauce thickens slightly, another 2 minutes.

Serve immediately with thinly sliced scallions on top.

Store leftovers in an airtight container in the fridge for up to 3 days.

NOTES

- If you can't find chow mein noodles in your grocery store, you can substitute sweet potato noodles, rice noodles, or soba noodles.
- If you're using reduced-sodium soy sauce in this recipe, you may need to season with a pinch of salt at the end. Taste the chow mein before you serve it and adjust the seasoning as necessary.

Left: Curry Crab Fried Rice
Right: Jerk Pork Chow Mein

CHINESE FOOD IN JAMAICA

The first Chinese who came to Jamaica arrived as indentured laborers in 1854, trying to escape political upheaval, opium wars, and floods that had wiped out food supplies in China. Their lives in Jamaica weren't much better, if at all. In the 1920s a second wave of Chinese immigrants came to the island, most of them businesspeople who quickly established themselves as experts in retail. By the 1950s, Chinese had set up hundreds of shops, especially grocery stores and restaurants.

They had brought with them from China only a handful of ingredients that could survive the long journey, soy sauce, dried noodles, and five-spice powder among them. These have since become staples in Jamaican cuisine. Unable to replace their core ingredients, the Chinese cooks made do with what was locally available, resulting in unique variations of traditional Chinese dishes. Tamarind replaced sour plums in a Chinese duck dish, and Scotch bonnet peppers were added to sweet and sour pork. Local produce like callaloo and okra showed up in stir-fries, and Jamaican curry found a home in Chinese fried rice.

One dish has become unique to Jamaican Chinese cuisine: suey mein (or sui mein), a flavorful soup that combines noodles, shrimp, vegetables, and Cantonese-style roast pork in a rich broth garnished with Scotch bonnet sauce and mushroom soy sauce.

Chinese immigrants also influenced Jamaican cooking: Where would we be without the rice they introduced to us?

OXTAIL AND DUMPLINGS

Serves 4

For the gnocchi

1½ cups (450 g) ricotta cheese, drained (see Notes)

2 large eggs, lightly beaten

1 cup (85 g) freshly grated Parmesan cheese

Kosher salt

1½ to 2 cups (180 to 240 g) tipo "00" flour or all-purpose flour, plus more for dusting

Extra-virgin olive oil (optional)

For the oxtail

3 tablespoons extra-virgin olive oil

3 garlic cloves, minced

Leaves from 3 thyme sprigs

1 small onion, diced

2 cups sliced shiitake or button mushrooms (about 4 ounces/115 g)

2 to 3 cups (about 125 g) leftover oxtail meat, pulled off the bones

1 cup (250 ml) heavy cream

½ cup (40 g) freshly grated Parmesan cheese, plus more for serving

2 handfuls arugula or spinach (optional)

Kosher salt and freshly ground black pepper

This is a fresh take on a traditional Jamaican oxtail recipe and an even fresher take on gnocchi. It uses leftover oxtail—if there is such a thing—and homemade ricotta gnocchi, which are the "dumplings" in this dish. If you don't have leftover oxtail, follow the instructions for cooking oxtail in the Oxtail and Butter Beans recipe on page 163, and once it has cooled, pull the meat off the bones for use in this recipe. Your efforts will be rewarded with tender, flavorful oxtail meat and pillowy gnocchi (see Notes) in a creamy, dreamy mushroom and parmesan sauce.

Make the gnocchi: In a large bowl, stir together the drained ricotta, eggs, Parmesan, and 1 teaspoon kosher salt. Add 1½ cups (180 g) of the flour and stir with a silicone spatula until a smooth but slightly sticky dough forms. Knead the dough in the bowl until smooth; if it's sticky at all, add more flour, a little at a time, being careful not to add too much extra so the dough doesn't get tough.

Dust some flour onto a work surface and turn the dough out onto it. Cut the dough into 4 equal portions and roll each into a log about 1 inch (2.5 cm) thick. If the dough is sticking to your work surface, dust it with a little more flour. Cut the logs into 1-inch (2.5 cm) pieces, then press each piece gently with the tines of a fork to indent it—this will help the gnocchi/dumpling soak up more sauce. Dust a sheet pan with a little flour and transfer the gnocchi onto it until you're ready to cook them. It takes some time to shape the gnocchi and you don't want them to get sticky while you're making the entire batch.

Bring a large pot of heavily salted water to a boil over high heat. Once the water is boiling, add the gnocchi and cook until all the pieces begin to float, 1 to 3 minutes. Scoop out about ½ cup (125 ml) of the cooking water and set it aside for the sauce. Drain the gnocchi and set them aside until you're ready to add them to the sauce. You may need to toss the cooked gnocchi in a little olive oil to prevent them from sticking together if your sauce isn't ready yet.

Cook the oxtail: Heat the olive oil in a large skillet over medium heat. Add the garlic, thyme, and onion and cook until the onions are translucent and fragrant, about 3 minutes.

Reduce the heat to medium-low. Add the mushrooms and cook until they are softened and starting to brown slightly, another 3 to 5 minutes, stirring frequently so you don't burn the onions.

Increase the heat to medium. Add the oxtail meat and cook until hot, then add ¼ cup (60 ml) of the cooking water from the gnocchi and the heavy cream. Reduce the heat to medium-low, bring to a simmer, and cook until the sauce starts to thicken, about 3 minutes. If the sauce is too thick—it should be loose enough to coat the dumplings—add more of the cooking water from the gnocchi, 1 tablespoon at a time, until it is the right consistency.

Add the cooked gnocchi and Parmesan to the sauce and stir gently until the Parmesan melts into the sauce and the gnocchi are well coated.

Fold in the arugula (if using) and cook until it is wilted, another minute or so. Season to taste with salt and pepper. Serve immediately with extra Parmesan on top.

Store leftovers in an airtight container in the fridge for up to 3 days. Reheat leftovers in a covered skillet over low heat with a splash of water to loosen the sauce.

NOTES

- If you don't want to make gnocchi from scratch, you can use a 1-pound (450 g) package of store-bought gnocchi, or any other pasta, cooked according to the package directions.
- To drain the ricotta, place it in a fine-mesh sieve and let the liquid drain for about 20 minutes. Alternatively, spread the ricotta in a thin layer between a few layers of paper towel on a plate, and press firmly with your hands to remove the excess liquid.

COFFEE-COCOA LAMB CHOPS

Serves 3 or 4

¼ cup (60 ml) extra-virgin olive oil, plus more for cooking

1 tablespoon finely ground coffee beans

1 tablespoon kosher salt

2 teaspoons unsweetened cocoa powder

2 teaspoons light brown sugar

1 teaspoon garlic powder

1 teaspoon onion powder

½ teaspoon freshly ground black pepper

½ teaspoon smoked paprika

½ teaspoon cayenne pepper

¼ teaspoon ground allspice

¼ teaspoon dried thyme

1 rack of lamb (2 pounds/900 g), divided into single chops

For the sauce

2 tablespoons (1 ounce/30 g) unsalted butter

Leaves from 2 thyme sprigs, chopped

Needles from 1 rosemary sprig, chopped

1 shallot, minced

The unique combination of coffee and cocoa pairs wonderfully with the rich, gamey taste of lamb, creating a dish that is both quick to prepare and incredibly flavorful. Its complex notes will surprise you. Perfect for impressing guests or elevating a weeknight meal, this recipe delivers a memorable dining experience with minimal effort. And if you're looking for the perfect drink to pair with this, try an iced Hibiscus "Rumgroni" (page 292).

In a small bowl, combine the olive oil, ground coffee, salt, cocoa powder, brown sugar, garlic powder, onion powder, black pepper, smoked paprika, cayenne, allspice, and thyme in a small bowl.

Pat the lamb chops dry with paper towels, then rub the marinade onto each of the chops to evenly coat. Place them in a bowl, cover, and marinate in the fridge for 30 to 60 minutes.

Preheat the oven to 400°F (200°C). Line a sheet pan with parchment paper or foil.

Heat a large skillet over medium-high heat, then drizzle a little oil in the pan. Working in batches, sear the lamb chops until lightly browned, 1 to 2 minutes per side, then transfer them to the lined sheet pan.

Roast until the lamb reaches your preferred doneness, 4 to 5 minutes for medium. Remove from the oven and let rest for 5 minutes before serving.

Meanwhile, make the sauce: Melt the butter in a small saucepan over medium heat, then add the thyme, rosemary, shallot, and garlic. Cook until the shallots are soft and fragrant, about 2 minutes.

1 garlic clove, minced

½ cup (125 ml) dry red wine

½ cup (125 ml) chicken stock

½ cup (110 g) guava jelly or apricot jelly

2 tablespoons apple cider vinegar

Kosher salt and freshly ground black pepper

Increase the heat to high, add the red wine, and cook until reduced by half, about 2 minutes. Add the chicken stock, guava jelly, and vinegar and cook until syrupy, another 8 minutes or so. Season to taste with salt and pepper.

Spoon the sauce over the coffee-cocoa lamb chops and serve immediately.

SOUP
JERK PORK
JERK CHICKEN
STEAM FISH
LOBSTER

JERK HONEY BUTTER STEAK

Serves 2

For the steak

One 12- to 16-ounce (340 to 450 g) steak (see Note)

2 tablespoons jerk marinade, homemade (page 315) or store-bought, or 1 tablespoon Dry Jerk Rub (page 317)

1 teaspoon kosher salt

For the jerk honey butter

4 tablespoons (2 ounces/60 g) unsalted butter, at room temperature

2 teaspoons jerk marinade, homemade (page 315) or store-bought

2 teaspoons honey

Grated zest of 1 lime

Kosher salt

To finish

1 tablespoon extra-virgin olive oil

This jerk honey butter steak brings sweet Jamaican heat to a classic steak. The recipe offers the option of a quick dry rub or a brief marinade to infuse the steak with the distinctive notes of jerk seasoning. Pair it with My Favorite Salad (page 148) or the Plantain and Black Bean Salad (page 155) to balance the spiciness with a touch of citrus, or enjoy it as a stand-alone main that showcases the depth of jerk flavor in every bite.

Prepare the steak: Pat the steak dry with paper towels, then season with the jerk marinade or dry jerk rub and salt. For the best flavor, marinate the steak in the fridge for at least 25 minutes or up to 2 hours.

Meanwhile, make the jerk honey butter: Place the butter, jerk marinade, honey, lime zest, and salt to taste in a small bowl and mix thoroughly with a fork or silicone spatula.

To finish: Heat a large cast-iron skillet over medium-high heat. As soon as the pan starts to smoke lightly, pour in the oil. Add the seasoned steak to the skillet and sear until it is nicely browned, 3 to 4 minutes per side, depending on your desired doneness. In the last minute or two of searing the steak, add 2 tablespoons of the jerk honey butter to the pan and, once the butter has melted, spoon it over the steak.

Transfer the steak to a cutting board and let rest for 5 to 8 minutes before slicing ½ inch (1 cm) thick. Serve immediately with extra jerk honey butter and another sprinkle of salt, if desired.

NOTE: Rib-eye or New York strip steak is best for this recipe, though you can use your preferred cut of steak and adjust the cooking time as necessary.

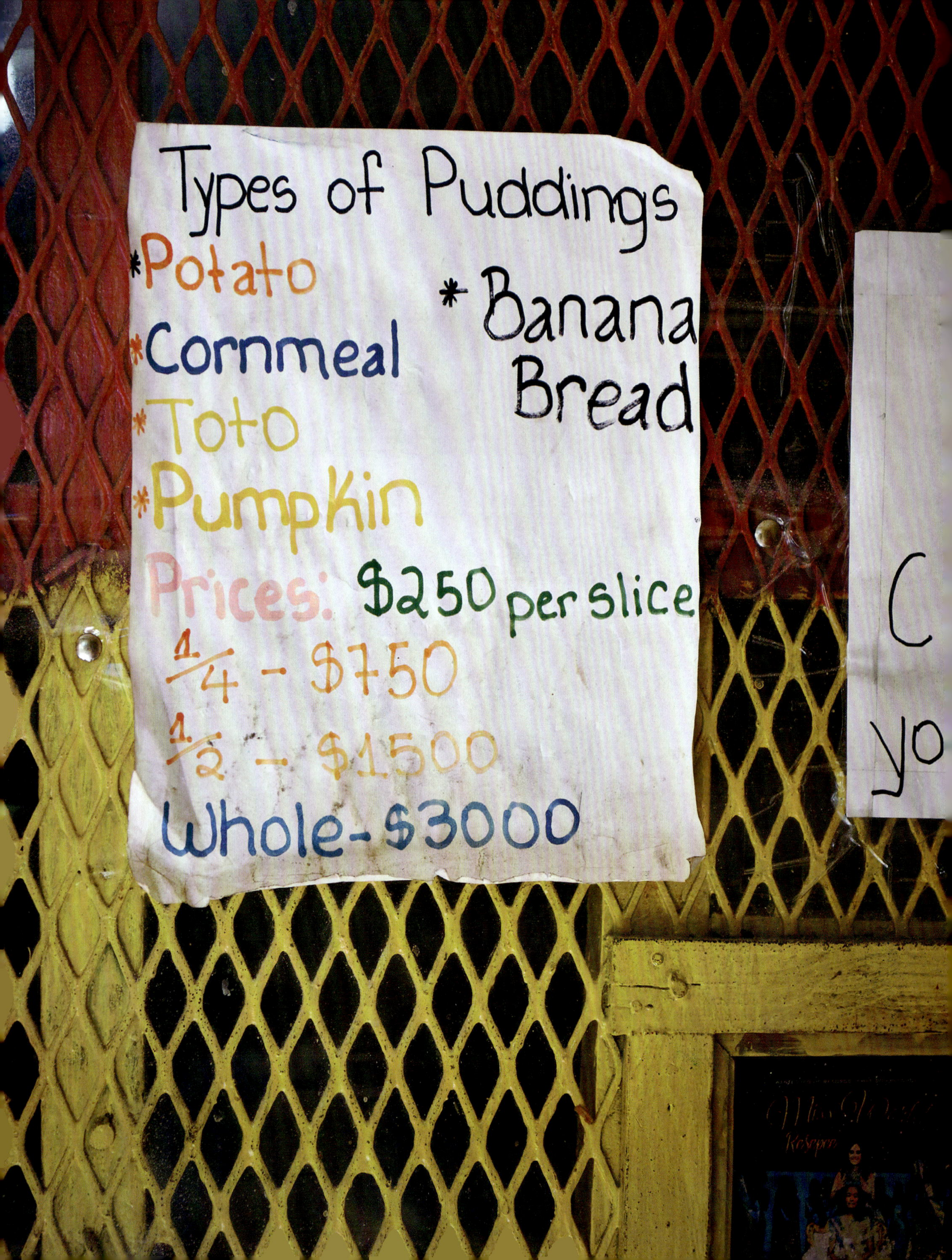
Types of Puddings
*Potato
*Cornmeal
*Toto
*Pumpkin
* Banana Bread
Prices: $250 per slice
1/4 - $750
1/2 - $1500
Whole - $3000

BRAWTA

DESSERTS

Brawta is the Jamaican word for "a little extra." Like when you order a latte and the barista tosses in a free cookie. Or when you go to the farmers' market and ask for a pound of onions and they throw in a handful of free garlic just because. Brawta is a bonus. It's the icing on the cake.

Dessert has always been a brawta for me. When I was younger, we couldn't afford to have a sweet every night after dinner, so when we did it was a gift. I have since learned that dessert is more than just a treat at the end of a meal. It's practically medicine. Sweets can boost your mood and reduce your stress. Dessert can bring nostalgia and comfort, like my mother's sweet potato pudding. Dessert is also a chance to practice mindfulness—an opportunity to be fully present and savor the moment. Think: ice cream and the satisfying crunch of a chocolate-dipped shell, or the rich, velvety texture of a freshly baked rum cake as it melts in your mouth. This chapter includes traditional Jamaican desserts like Gizzada, Spice Bun, and Jamaican Fruit Cake, as well as a few modern takes on classic flavors, such as Rum Cake Tiramisu.

PATSY'S SWEET POTATO PUDDING

Makes two 8-inch (20 cm) round puddings

½ cup (80 g) raisins (optional)

¼ cup (60 ml) dark rum (optional)

Softened butter, for the pans

3 large red-skinned sweet potatoes (2 pounds/900 g total), peeled and cut into 1-inch (2.5 cm) cubes

2 small taro roots (aka coco; 8 ounces/225 g total)

Two 14-ounce (400 ml) cans coconut milk (3½ cups)

2 cups (440 g) packed dark brown sugar

8 tablespoons (4 ounces/115 g) unsalted butter, melted

3 tablespoons pure vanilla extract

½ teaspoon almond extract

1 cup (140 g) fine yellow cornmeal

1 tablespoon ground cinnamon

2 teaspoons freshly grated nutmeg

2 teaspoons baking powder

2 teaspoons kosher salt

This very traditional dessert is fondly referred to in Jamaica as "hell a top, hell a bottom, and hallelujah in the middle," a phrase that describes how it's baked—in a Dutch oven buried in the glowing embers of a coal stove, with more glowing coals and ash heaped on top of the lid for insulation. This version is baked in the oven.

The type of sweet potato you use in this recipe is crucial. Look for the pink-skinned, white-fleshed variety we use in Jamaica (see Pantry, page 23). Darker-fleshed sweet potatoes have a high water content that results in a sludgy (instead of sliceable) pudding. This is my mother's recipe, and she always used taro root, though yam (see page 26) also works. There's no flour in this recipe, so yes, it's also gluten-free!

If you're using raisins, place them in a small bowl, pour over the rum, and soak overnight to rehydrate the raisins. (Alternatively, bring the raisins and rum to a simmer in a small saucepan over medium heat, then turn off the heat and let sit for 30 minutes.)

Preheat the oven to 350°F (180°C). Grease two 8-inch (20 cm) round cake pans with butter.

In a blender, combine the sweet potatoes, taro, and 3 cups (750 ml) of the coconut milk. Blend on high speed until smooth. There should be no chunks of sweet potato left. Pour the mixture into a large bowl and stir in 1½ cups (330 g) of the brown sugar, the melted butter, 2 tablespoons of the vanilla, and the almond extract.

In a separate bowl, whisk together the cornmeal, cinnamon, nutmeg, baking powder, and salt. Add the dry ingredients to the blended sweet potato mixture and mix well to combine. Gently fold in the soaked raisins and rum (if using), then pour the batter into the prepared pans.

Bake the puddings for 45 minutes to 1 hour, until the centers just start to set.

Meanwhile, in a bowl, whisk together the remaining ½ cup (125 ml) coconut milk, ½ cup (110 g) brown sugar, and 1 tablespoon vanilla.

Once the tops of the puddings just start to set, pour the coconut milk mixture over them, dividing it equally between them, and bake for another 30 minutes.

Let cool for at least 30 minutes, then run a knife around the edge of the puddings and serve warm.

Store in an airtight container in the fridge for up to 1 week. Leftovers can be eaten cold or warmed briefly in the microwave.

GIZZADA

Makes 8 tarts

For the pastry

2 cups (250 g) all-purpose flour

2 tablespoons granulated sugar

1 teaspoon kosher salt

¼ teaspoon freshly grated nutmeg

4 tablespoons (2 ounces/60 g) cold unsalted butter, cubed

¼ to ⅓ cup (60 to 80 ml) ice-cold water

For the coconut filling

3 cups (360 g) sweetened shredded coconut

1 cup (220 g) packed light brown sugar

2 teaspoons pure vanilla extract

2 teaspoons grated fresh ginger

1 teaspoon ground cinnamon

½ teaspoon freshly grated nutmeg

½ teaspoon kosher salt

1 tablespoon (0.5 ounce/15 g) butter

For assembly

Egg wash (optional): 1 egg, lightly beaten

In the late fifteenth and early sixteenth centuries, Portuguese Jews fleeing the Spanish Inquisition sought refuge in Jamaica, among other places in the New World. They established communities where they could practice their faith freely and brought with them various cultural traditions, including culinary ones. One such tradition was a pastry known as *queijadas de Sintra*, mini tarts with a sweet, cheesy filling. Over time, this dessert evolved in Jamaica into gizzada, a tart shell filled with a sweet, spiced coconut mixture. This adaptation of queijadas de Sintra reflects how Jewish heritage blended with Jamaican ingredients and flavors, creating a dessert that remains a testament to Jamaica's diverse cultural history.

Make the pastry: In a medium bowl, whisk together the flour, granulated sugar, salt, and nutmeg. Add the cubed butter and use your fingers or a fork to work the butter into the flour until the mixture resembles coarse crumbs. Slowly add the water and knead gently in the bowl with your hands to form a firm dough—it shouldn't be crumbly at this stage—being careful not to overwork the dough or the pastry won't be as flaky. Wrap the ball of dough with plastic wrap and let it rest in the fridge for at least 30 minutes.

Make the coconut filling: In a medium saucepan, stir together 1 cup (250 ml) water, the shredded coconut, brown sugar, vanilla, ginger, cinnamon, nutmeg, and salt. Cook over medium-high heat until the sugar dissolves and the liquid comes to a boil. Continue to cook, stirring occasionally, until the coconut mixture is thick and syrupy and most of the liquid has evaporated, 10 to 15 minutes.

Remove from the heat and stir in the butter. Set aside and let cool, or you can spread the mixture onto a plate or tray to cool it faster.

Assemble the gizzadas: Preheat the oven to 350°F (180°C). Line a sheet pan with parchment paper.

Unwrap the dough and cut it into 8 equal portions, then roll each portion into a ball. Using a rolling pin, roll each ball of dough into a round about ¼ inch (6 mm) thick. If you want more uniform tarts, trim the edges of each dough round with a round cookie cutter. Fold up the outside edge of each round of dough, crimping the edge with your fingers as you go, to form a tart shell that is 3 to 4 inches (8 to 10 cm) in diameter. Repeat until you've shaped all 8 rounds of dough. Place the tart shells on the prepared sheet pan and use a fork to poke holes in the base of each tart shell.

Bake for 8 to 10 minutes, until the pastry has just started to cook. Remove from the oven and fill each tart shell with about ¼ cup (60 g) of the cooled coconut mixture. For a golden-brown pastry, brush the edges of the tart shells with the egg wash, if desired. Then return them to the oven and bake until the gizzadas are lightly browned on top, 15 to 20 minutes. Remove from the oven and let cool before serving.

Store in an airtight container at room temperature for up to 4 days.

Left: Gizzada
Right: Peanut Drops

PEANUT DROPS

Makes 8 to 12

2 cups (225 g) roasted peanuts (see Notes)

1½ cups (300 g) raw cane sugar or light brown sugar

2 tablespoons grated fresh ginger

1 tablespoon pure vanilla extract

½ teaspoon ground cinnamon

¼ teaspoon freshly grated nutmeg

¼ teaspoon kosher salt (see Notes)

Peanut drops are a classic sweet treat with a perfect balance of crispy and chewy. This recipe is a great introduction to candy-making because it hinges on a simple yet precise process of sugar caramelization. The core of this recipe is achieving the right consistency for the sugar syrup—a step that requires patience and close attention. Stirring constantly is crucial to prevent the sugar from burning, and a heavy-bottomed saucepan is recommended to ensure even heat distribution and prevent hot spots that could scorch the sugar. Adding the aromatics—vanilla, cinnamon, and nutmeg—toward the end of cooking helps retain their flavors, which would otherwise dissipate if added too early.

The reward for all your hard work: gingery and chewy, crunchy-on-the-outside peanut drops that capture the essence of traditional Caribbean sweets.

Line a sheet pan with parchment paper and set near the stove. In a large heavy-bottomed saucepan, combine the peanuts, sugar, ginger, and 1 cup (250 ml) water and bring to a boil over medium-high heat, stirring frequently.

Reduce the heat to medium and cook, stirring frequently so the sugar doesn't burn, until the mixture starts to thicken and becomes thick like caramel, 30 to 35 minutes.

Once the liquid has reduced and the peanuts are fully coated in the thick caramel, reduce the heat to low and stir in the vanilla, cinnamon, nutmeg, and salt.

Working quickly so the mixture doesn't harden, use a large spoon to drop clusters of the peanut mixture onto the prepared sheet pan. Each drop should have 2 to 3 tablespoons of the mixture. The mixture will be extremely hot—work carefully so you don't burn yourself.

Let the peanut drops cool for at least 30 minutes to harden (see Notes), then enjoy.

Store in an airtight container at room temperature for up to 1 week.

NOTES

- You can use either salted or unsalted peanuts for this recipe. If your peanuts aren't roasted, spread them on a sheet pan and bake at 350°F (180°C) until the peanuts are golden brown, 6 to 8 minutes.
- For a less traditional variation of these peanut drops, substitute unsweetened coconut flakes, pumpkin seeds, cashews, or almonds for up to 1 cup (110 g) of the peanuts.
- If using salted peanuts, omit the salt.
- If the drops don't set, it means you didn't reduce the liquid enough to cook out the water. Place them back in a saucepan with 2 tablespoons brown sugar and cook until thick and syrupy. Spoon them onto a sheet pan with a fresh sheet of parchment and let cool before enjoying.

PEANUTS AREN'T JUST FOR SNACKING

Peanuts originated in South America and were introduced to Africa via Portuguese explorers in the sixteenth century. Peanuts were brought to Jamaica as a food for enslaved people and have been grown on the island ever since. Jamaican peanut porridge is a popular breakfast option, made from blended peanuts, coconut milk, spices like cinnamon and nutmeg, and condensed milk or sugar for sweetener. And, of course, there are Peanut Drops (see recipe above) and Peanut Punch (page 295), a rich, creamy peanut drink.

Unlike almonds or walnuts, which grow on trees, peanuts grow underground and are a legume. They're packed with protein, fiber, and healthy fats, making them a great choice for a filling snack or meal. Peanuts are also budget-friendly and eco-friendly, using far less water to grow than almonds, and as a bonus they help enrich the soil by fixing nitrogen from the air.

RUM AND RAISIN BREAD PUDDING

Serves 8

For the pudding

3 tablespoons (1.5 ounces/ 45 g) unsalted butter, plus more to grease the pan

6 cups stale challah or brioche (see Notes), cut into 1-inch (2.5 cm) cubes

2 cups (500 ml) whole milk

1 cup (250 ml) heavy cream

¾ cup (165 g) packed light brown sugar

4 large eggs

¼ cup (60 ml) dark rum

2 tablespoons pure vanilla extract

1 teaspoon ground cinnamon

½ teaspoon kosher salt

½ cup (80 g) raisins

For the rum sauce

2 tablespoons (1 ounce/ 30 g) unsalted butter

2 tablespoons all-purpose flour

1 cup (250 ml) heavy cream

1 cup (250 ml) whole milk

½ cup (110 g) packed light brown sugar

¼ cup (60 ml) dark rum

1 tablespoon pure vanilla extract

¼ teaspoon freshly grated nutmeg

¼ teaspoon kosher salt

Bread pudding is not the soggy, bland, old man's dessert I used to think it was. Trust me, this one is a game changer. It's rich, buttery, and just the right amount of boozy. The sweetness is spot on, and bread pudding couldn't be easier to make. No fancy ingredients, no complicated steps—just a comforting dessert that's perfect for sharing. Infused with dark rum, rich vanilla, and warm spices, this rum and raisin bread pudding is deeply flavorful, moist, and luxurious. The velvety rum sauce poured over the top brings an extra layer of indulgence.

Make the pudding: Preheat the oven to 350°F (180°C). Grease an 8-inch (20 cm) square baking dish with butter.

Add the cubed bread to the baking dish.

In a small saucepan, combine the milk, heavy cream, brown sugar, and butter and heat over medium-low heat until the milk just begins to bubble around the edges. Remove from the heat and set aside until the mixture is slightly warm, but not hot (you don't want to curdle the eggs).

Crack the eggs into a bowl and whisk them together. While whisking constantly, slowly pour in the milk mixture a little at a time to temper the eggs without cooking them. Once all the milk mixture has been added and the mixture is smooth, whisk in the rum, vanilla, cinnamon, and salt.

Pour the mixture evenly over the bread in the baking dish, making sure all the pieces are covered with the liquid. Spread the raisins evenly over the top of the bread pudding, tucking some in between the pieces of bread. Gently press the top of the bread pudding to allow the custard to soak into all the pieces of bread. Let the pudding sit for 10 minutes.

recipe continues

Bake for 40 to 45 minutes (see Notes), until the top is golden brown and the center no longer jiggles. Remove from the oven and let cool before serving.

Meanwhile, make the rum sauce: In a small saucepan, melt the butter over low heat. Add the flour and cook, stirring constantly, until a thick paste forms, about 1 minute.

Slowly add the heavy cream and milk, whisking constantly to prevent lumps from forming. Add the brown sugar, rum, vanilla, nutmeg, and salt and whisk to combine. Increase the heat to medium-low and cook, stirring constantly, until the sauce is thick enough to coat the back of a spoon, about 5 minutes. Turn off the heat and set aside to cool slightly.

Serve the warm rum sauce drizzled over the top of the bread pudding.

Store the bread pudding and rum sauce in separate airtight containers in the fridge for up to 5 days. Warm leftover bread pudding in the microwave or oven.

NOTES

- Brioche or challah bread are best for this recipe, though a good white bread will do just fine. Or you can make this gluten-free by using gluten-free bread (in which case, use gluten-free flour to make the rum sauce). Avoid using breads that are crusty.

- If you're using fresh bread (bread that's been baked within the last two days), dry it out before assembling the bread pudding by spreading the cubes onto a sheet pan and baking for 10 minutes at 275°F (130°C), or until dry. This will help the bread absorb the custard better.

- If the bread pudding starts to burn on top before it's finished baking, cover it with foil and continue to bake until cooked through.

SPICE BUN

Makes 1 loaf

Softened butter, for the pan

3 cups (375 g) all-purpose flour

1 tablespoon baking powder

1 tablespoon ground cinnamon

1 teaspoon freshly grated nutmeg

1 teaspoon ground ginger

1 teaspoon kosher salt

½ teaspoon ground allspice

1 bottle (375 ml) stout (1½ cups), preferably Guinness

1 cup (220 g) packed light brown sugar

5 tablespoons (2.5 ounces/70 g) butter, melted

¼ cup (60 g) guava jam (see Notes)

1 tablespoon molasses

1 tablespoon pure vanilla extract

1 large egg, lightly beaten

1 cup (160 g) raisins (see Notes)

1 tablespoon honey

1 tablespoon hot water

Slice of sharp Cheddar or butter, for serving (optional)

There are a few things you should know about spice bun before you make it. The first is that it's not a bun, it's a loaf. The second thing is that we call it simply "bun" in Jamaica. And finally, bun is rarely eaten without cheese (a very specific cheese: the salty-smooth Tastee Cheese), because bun and cheese just go together, like bread and butter or spaghetti and meatballs.

This spiced loaf is a year-round Jamaican favorite that perfectly exemplifies the island's knack for taking something good and making it better. With its origins linked to British hot cross buns, Jamaican bun evolved through the clever use of local ingredients and flavors. This dense, fragrant loaf is enriched with dark stout and molasses and studded with raisins. Around Easter, candied cherries and citrus peel are added. The result is a sweet, moist loaf that pairs irresistibly with Tastee Cheese, though a sharp Cheddar will do in a pinch, or even a thick layer of butter (or both!).

Preheat the oven to 350°F (180°C). Grease a 9-by-5-inch (23 by 13 cm) loaf pan with butter.

Sift the flour into a large bowl along with the baking powder, cinnamon, nutmeg, ginger, salt, and allspice. Whisk together and set aside.

In a separate bowl, whisk together the beer, brown sugar, ¼ cup (60 ml) of the melted butter, the guava jam, molasses, vanilla, and egg. Add the dry ingredients to the liquid mixture and stir with a silicone spatula until combined, making sure there are no lumps in the batter. Add the raisins to the batter and fold them in with the spatula. Pour the batter into the prepared loaf pan.

Bake for 30 minutes. Reduce the heat to 325°F (160°F) and bake for another 30 minutes, or until a toothpick inserted in the center comes out clean.

recipe continues

While the bun bakes, in a small bowl, combine the remaining 1 tablespoon melted butter, honey, and hot water to make a glaze.

As soon as the bun comes out of the oven, use a pastry brush to paint the top with the glaze, then let it cool. Once the bun has cooled, remove it from the loaf pan, slice, and enjoy on its own or with slices of Cheddar or butter, if desired.

Store in an airtight container, unsliced, at room temperature for up to 4 days.

NOTES

- You can use strawberry jam instead of guava jam in this recipe. The jam adds moisture to the bun.
- For added flavor and extra-juicy raisins, soak the raisins overnight in enough rum to cover them, or simmer them in rum for 5 minutes to rehydrate them. Drain the rum off and add the drunken raisins to the recipe.

JAMAICAN FRUIT CAKE

(CHRISTMAS PUDDING)

Makes three 8-inch (20 cm) round puddings

2 pounds (900 g) dark raisins

1 pound (450 g) golden raisins

1 pound (450 g) pitted prunes

1 pound (450 g) dried currants

4 cups (1 L) overproof white rum, preferably Wray & Nephew

3 cups (750 ml) sweet red wine (see Notes)

Softened butter, for the cake pans

1 pound (450 g) unsalted butter, at room temperature

3 cups (660 g) packed light brown sugar

10 large eggs

¼ cup (60 ml) browning

3 tablespoons pure vanilla extract

4 cups (500 g) all-purpose flour, sifted

4 teaspoons baking powder

1 teaspoon ground cinnamon

1 teaspoon freshly grated nutmeg

1 teaspoon kosher salt

½ teaspoon ground allspice

1 cup (250 ml) dark rum (optional), for finishing

Jamaican fruit cake has many aliases: Christmas cake, black cake, even Christmas pudding. It also has deep historical and cultural roots that reflect the Caribbean's colonial past. It is widely believed that the dessert is a descendant of British plum pudding recipes brought to the Caribbean by colonizers in the eighteenth century. Over time, the recipe has been adapted to incorporate indigenous ingredients like dark rum, molasses, and spices, giving the cake its distinctive rich flavor and dark color. The result is a dense, moist cake, with dried fruits that may have been marinating in rum for months, so plan ahead if you can!

In a large bowl, combine the dark raisins, golden raisins, prunes, and currants. Stir in the rum and wine, then transfer the fruit and alcohol to a large jar or other large container with a lid. Let the fruit soak for at least 5 days and up to a whole year, if you wish (see Notes).

Once the fruit has soaked and softened, transfer the fruit and the soaking liquid to a blender or food processor and blend until a smooth paste forms. You'll likely need to work in batches for this depending on the size of your blender. Set the blended fruit/alcohol mixture aside.

Preheat the oven to 300°F (150°C). Line the bottom of three 8-inch (20 cm) round cake pans (see Notes) with rounds of parchment paper, then grease the bottom and sides of the pans with butter. Set aside.

In the largest bowl you can find, cream the butter and brown sugar together with a hand mixer until smooth and fluffy, 6 to 8 minutes on high speed (see Notes). Add the eggs one at a time, beating well after each addition. Blend until all the eggs are incorporated and the mixture is smooth. Add the browning and vanilla and mix again.

recipe continues

In a separate bowl, whisk together the sifted flour, baking powder, cinnamon, nutmeg, salt, and allspice.

Add about half the flour mixture to the bowl with the butter mixture and mix until just combined. Add about half the blended fruit mixture to the bowl and mix again until just combined. Repeat this process until you've incorporated all the flour and blended fruit. The batter should be thick and without lumps.

Divide the cake batter among the prepared pans. Place the filled pans into the oven (see Notes) and bake for 20 minutes. Reduce the oven temperature to 250°F (120°C) and bake for another 2 to 3 hours, or until a cake tester in the center comes out clean.

Remove the cakes from the oven. Brush the tops with dark rum (if using) while they cool. Continue to brush the cakes every 20 minutes or so until you've used up all the rum.

Store wrapped tightly in plastic wrap or foil in a cool, dark place for up to 1 month—in fact, this cake is better after a few days.

NOTES

- Port wine adds a nice flavor to these puddings, but you can use your favorite sweet red wine. If all you have is dry white wine, add ¼ cup (50 g) sugar to the wine before you use it.
- If you're in a pinch and you didn't get the chance to soak the fruit, add the dried fruit to a large saucepan along with the red wine and white rum. Simmer over medium-low heat until the fruit has softened and absorbed some of the alcohol. Let cool before using in the recipe.
- You can make this recipe in disposable aluminum cake pans as well—this is a great idea if you plan to gift a cake or two to family or friends.
- If you prefer to use a stand mixer, work in batches and use the paddle attachment.
- For a moister cake, place a shallow pan of water at the bottom of the oven while baking.
- If you want to do it the traditional way, start soaking your fruits in January for baking in December.

TORTUGA-STYLE RUM CAKE

Makes one 9-inch (23 cm) Bundt cake

For the rum cake

Softened butter and flour, for the pan

2½ cups (315 g) all-purpose flour

¼ cup (30 g) cornstarch

2 teaspoons baking powder

1 teaspoon kosher salt

½ teaspoon baking soda

½ teaspoon freshly grated nutmeg

2 cups (400 g) sugar

8 ounces (225 g) unsalted butter, at room temperature

¼ cup (60 ml) vegetable oil or other neutral oil

4 large eggs, at room temperature

½ cup (125 ml) whole milk

¼ cup (60 ml) dark rum

1 tablespoon pure vanilla extract

For the rum glaze

1 cup (200 g) sugar

8 tablespoons (4 ounces/115 g) butter

½ cup (125 ml) dark rum

1 tablespoon pure vanilla extract

½ teaspoon kosher salt

Rum is central to Jamaica's story, but it's a story with some hard truths. Rum came out of the sugar plantations, with labor provided by enslaved Africans. Over time, though, we have made rum our own, turning it into a powerful, iconic symbol of our country. This rum cake is a great example of that. It's buttery, moist, and soaked in a deep, rich rum glaze that brings out all the best flavors. Simple ingredients come together here to make a dessert that's as bold and unforgettable as Jamaica itself. I learned how to make this cake at one of my earliest jobs as a young chef in training.

Make the rum cake: Preheat the oven to 325°F (160°C). Butter and flour a 9-inch (23 cm) Bundt pan.

Sift the flour, cornstarch, baking powder, salt, baking soda, and nutmeg into a medium bowl. Whisk together and set aside.

In a stand mixer fitted with the paddle, combine the sugar, butter, and vegetable oil and beat on high speed until fluffy and mostly smooth, 4 to 6 minutes. Reduce the speed to medium, then add the eggs one at a time, beating well after each addition. Add the milk, rum, and vanilla and continue to mix until just combined, another minute.

Add the flour mixture and mix on low speed until just combined. Scrape the sides of the bowl with a silicone spatula and mix again to ensure there are no pockets of flour in the batter. Spread the batter evenly in the prepared Bundt pan.

Bake for about 1 hour, or until a toothpick inserted into the center comes out clean.

Let the cake cool for 10 minutes, then use a skewer or toothpick to poke holes all over the exposed top of the cake.

recipe continues

Meanwhile, make the rum glaze: In a small saucepan, combine the sugar, butter, and 1 cup (250 ml) water and bring to a simmer over medium heat. Cook until the sugar has dissolved, about 3 minutes, stirring constantly. Remove from heat and stir in the rum, vanilla, and salt.

Carefully spoon half the rum glaze evenly over the cake in the pan and let the cake absorb it. Once the glaze has been absorbed, invert the cake onto a serving plate and poke more holes all over the surface of the cake with the same skewer or toothpick. Spoon the rest of the glaze over the top of the cake, working slowly so the cake can absorb all the glaze.

The cake can be sliced and served immediately or stored at room temperature in an airtight container for up to 3 days.

NOTE: Use any leftover rum cake (is this a thing, though?) to make Rum Cake Tiramisu (page 259).

THE STORY OF JAMAICAN RUM

Dunder. Funk. Muck. These are words from the dictionary of Jamaican rum.

At its most basic, rum is a by-product of sugar production. To make sugar, you squeeze the juice out of sugarcane stalks and boil the cane juice until crystals form and precipitate out. What's left after crystallization is molasses, a thick, almost black, slightly bitter syrup. In its early days molasses was often dumped or used to feed slaves or cattle. And then someone—we're not sure who—discovered that molasses could be fermented into a cane wine, which could be distilled into rum.

Early versions of rum were crude, harsh, and not for the faint of heart. Jamaican rum became more refined in 1749 with the establishment of Appleton Estate, one of the oldest and best-known rum producers in the world. Appleton transformed demon water into a sophisticated and prized spirit. Rum became so popular that by the late nineteenth century there were more than one hundred distilleries in Jamaica. When slavery ended and production costs went up, almost all of them were forced to shut down. There are now just six distilleries on the island.

What makes Jamaican rum so special? I may be a little biased, but even rum experts who don't have any attachment to the island will tell you our rum is unique. Jamaican rum has what can best be described as robust and complex flavors. The words *funky* and *hogo* are tossed around a lot. *Hogo* comes from the French *haut goût*, which refers to a strong but desirable flavor, like gamey, slightly off meat. Today, *hogo* is used to describe the earthy, funky, rotting-fruit flavor in some rums. In Jamaica, this is partly due to the use of an all-natural, GMO-free strain of yeast in the fermentation process.

Distillation is usually done in traditional pot stills in Jamaica. Pot stills aren't very efficient at separating alcohol from other by-products, so the distillation takes longer, leaving the rum more full-bodied and flavorful. Some Jamaican distillers use dunder and muck to amp up a rum's complexity. Dunder is the liquid left over from a previous distillation. It boosts flavor and helps keep the fermentation consistent, like the sour mash process in bourbon. At some distilleries, the dunder is stored in a muck pit, where it breaks down with other waste and bacteria, creating a strong-flavored (some might say putrid) mix that's added in small amounts to the fermentation. This makes the rum even more funky.

There are other factors that influence the flavor of rum: the soil, the climate, growing conditions, harvesting and processing techniques, how the molasses is produced, and even the water. Jamaican rums are all made from molasses and use water that has been filtered through natural Jamaican limestone. Additives such as sugar, artificial flavors, or colors are not allowed.

The final step is the aging process. Jamaican rum is aged in oak barrels, where it soaks up flavors and color from the wood—caramel, spice, maybe vanilla. Once the rum has aged, master blenders combine rums to create a smooth, well-balanced final product.

Rum unites us—young and old, rich and poor, Jamaicans from every walk of life drink it. Rum is served in every restaurant, bar, dancehall, club, and hotel. But it's not just for drinking. We use it for cooking. We rub it on babies' heads to prevent colds. We use it to bless new construction and ward off evil spirits. We mix it with lime and honey to cure the flu. Rum feeds into the tourist version of Jamaica, but it is also a big part of the lived reality of the island. To know Jamaica, you need to understand our rum.

CHOCOLATE-DIPPED ICE CREAM BARS

Makes 8 ice cream bars

- 1 cup (160 g) raisins
- ½ cup (125 ml) dark rum
- 2 cups (500 ml) cold heavy whipping cream
- ¾ cup (180 ml) sweetened condensed milk
- 1 tablespoon pure vanilla extract or vanilla bean paste
- ¼ teaspoon ground cinnamon
- ¼ teaspoon freshly grated nutmeg
- ¼ teaspoon kosher salt
- 2 cups (about 480 g) dark chocolate chips
- ¼ cup (60 ml) coconut oil
- Optional toppings: flaky sea salt, sweetened shredded coconut, or chopped nuts (walnuts, pecans, almonds, peanuts, etc.)

Ice cream at Devon House was a rare Sunday treat for me and my siblings, and I've loved it ever since. When it comes to these rum and raisin ice cream bars, the magic is in the method. There's no ice cream maker needed here, just a simple no-churn technique that delivers the creamy, scoopable texture we all love. The trick is whipping the cream just right—stiff peaks but still smooth—so it blends perfectly with the sweetened condensed milk and spices. Add in rum-soaked raisins, and you've got a rich, rummy, perfect dessert. But it gets better: You're dipping the ice cream to make a silky chocolate shell that cracks just right when you bite into it. It's a fresh take on a classic flavor, perfect for impressing friends without spending all day in the kitchen.

In a small saucepan, combine the raisins and dark rum and bring to a low simmer over medium heat. Remove from the heat and let the raisins soak in the rum for 30 to 60 minutes. Drain the raisins, reserving ¼ cup (60 ml) of the rum.

In a stand mixer fitted with the whisk (see Notes), beat the whipping cream on high speed until stiff peaks form, 3 to 4 minutes.

In a separate bowl, whisk together the condensed milk, vanilla, cinnamon, nutmeg, and salt. Add the condensed milk mixture to the whipped cream, along with the raisins and the reserved ¼ cup (60 ml) rum, and gently fold in with a silicone spatula until just combined, being careful not to deflate the whipped cream.

Pour the mixture into a silicone ice cream bar mold (see Notes), then insert ice pop sticks into each of the bars. Freeze until solid, at least 8 hours.

In a microwave-safe bowl, microwave (see Notes) the chocolate and coconut oil in 30-second increments, stirring after each, until

melted. Let cool slightly, then transfer to a tall glass that's just wide enough to fit the ice cream bars.

Line a tray with parchment paper. Remove the ice cream bars from the mold and dip each one into the melted chocolate, working quickly so the ice cream doesn't melt. Place the chocolate-coated bars on the lined tray. Sprinkle the tops with any optional toppings and freeze again for at least 1 hour, until the chocolate is hard and the ice cream has firmed up again. Enjoy straight out of the freezer.

Wrap any leftover ice cream bars with parchment paper and store in an airtight container in the freezer for up to 1 month.

NOTES

- You can also use a hand mixer to whip the cream, but it will take a bit longer to reach stiff peaks, 5 to 6 minutes.

- If you don't have an ice cream bar mold, you can pour the mixture into an 8-inch (20 cm) square baking pan lined with parchment paper. Top the mixture with another sheet of parchment paper and freeze for 8 to 12 hours before cutting the ice cream into 8 rectangles. Insert ice pop sticks into the bottom of each bar once cut. You'll need to freeze the bars again before dipping them in chocolate so they don't melt.

- If you don't have a microwave, place the chocolate and coconut oil in a heatproof bowl over a large saucepan of simmering water and stir until melted, 3 to 4 minutes.

RUM CAKE TIRAMISU

Serves 8

6 egg yolks

1 cup (200 g) sugar

One 16-ounce (453 g) container mascarpone cheese (about 2 cups)

¾ cup (180 ml) dark rum (see Notes)

1 tablespoon pure vanilla extract

½ teaspoon kosher salt

2 cups (500 ml) heavy cream

2 cups (500 ml) brewed coffee or espresso, at room temperature

Half a leftover Tortuga-Style Rum Cake (page 251), cut into 1-inch (2.5 cm) cubes (see Notes)

Cocoa powder, for dusting

Let's pretend we live in a world where leftover rum cake is a thing. What do you do with the leftovers? You make rum cake tiramisu. This recipe takes the Italian classic and gives it a Caribbean twist. Instead of the usual ladyfingers soaked in coffee and liqueur, you'll layer chunks of rum cake that have been doused in a mix of rum and coffee. This swap adds a deeper, richer flavor with a bold hit of rum that really stands out. The mascarpone and whipped cream mixture stays true to the original tiramisu's silky texture, but the rum cake brings an extra layer of decadence and moisture to each bite.

Fill a medium saucepan with about 2 inches (5 cm) of water and set over medium heat. Place the egg yolks and sugar in a heatproof medium bowl and place the bowl over the saucepan, making sure it doesn't touch the water. Heat, whisking constantly, until the mixture is pale yellow and thick, 4 to 5 minutes.

Whisk in the mascarpone cheese, ¼ cup (60 ml) of the rum, the vanilla, and the salt. Whisk until the mixture is smooth, then remove from the heat and set aside to cool for at least 10 minutes.

While the egg mixture cools, in a stand mixer fitted with the whisk (or in a bowl with a hand mixer), beat the cream at medium-high speed until stiff peaks form.

Fold the whipped cream into the cooled egg mixture until fully incorporated, working gently to avoid deflating the whipped cream. Set aside until ready to assemble.

In a small bowl, stir the coffee and remaining ½ cup (120 ml) dark rum together.

Begin assembling the tiramisu in a 9-by-13-inch (23 by 33 cm) glass casserole dish or in 8 small bowls or jars. Spread some of the mascarpone mixture on the bottom of the dish, then dip a few pieces of cubed rum cake into the rum/coffee mixture and layer them on top

of the mascarpone mixture. Continue layering these components until you've used all the mascarpone mixture and the rum cake is finished, making sure that the top layer is the mascarpone mix. Cover with plastic wrap and refrigerate for at least 2 hours or up to overnight.

Sift some cocoa powder over the top before serving.

Store in an airtight container in the fridge for up to 5 days or in the freezer for up to 3 months. Thaw frozen tiramisu fully in the fridge for 1 day before enjoying.

NOTES

- You can replace up to ¼ cup (60 ml) of the dark rum with coffee liqueur if you want a stronger coffee flavor.
- If you do not have leftover rum cake, you can use store-bought pound cake that's been soaked in the rum glaze used in the Tortuga-Style Rum Cake (page 251).

CINNAMON ROLLS *with* STICKY COFFEE GLAZE

Makes 12 rolls

1 cup (250 ml) whole milk, warmed

One ¼-ounce envelope active dry yeast (2¼ teaspoons)

½ cup (100 g) plus 1 tablespoon granulated sugar

8 tablespoons (4 ounces/115 g) butter, melted

1 teaspoon kosher salt

½ teaspoon freshly grated nutmeg

1 large egg, lightly beaten

4 cups (500 g) bread flour (see Notes), plus more for dusting

Oil, for the dough-rising bowl

Softened butter, for the baking pan

For the filling

½ cup (110 g) packed light brown sugar

4 tablespoons (2 ounces/60 g) butter, at room temperature

2 tablespoons ground cinnamon

½ cup (125 ml) heavy cream, for brushing

ingredients continue

There is nothing sweeter than the smell of freshly baked cinnamon rolls in the morning . . . except freshly baked cinnamon rolls *and* coffee! These cinnamon rolls take a classic favorite to the next level with a sticky coffee glaze that perfectly complements the warmth of cinnamon. You will need plenty of counter space to roll out the dough, and plenty of flour for dusting so your dough doesn't stick to the surface.

In the bowl of a stand mixer, stir together the warm milk, yeast, and 1 tablespoon of the sugar. Let the mixture sit until slightly foamy, about 5 minutes. Add the melted butter, remaining ½ cup (100 g) sugar, the salt, nutmeg, and egg and whisk to combine. Sift the flour into the bowl with a fine-mesh sieve, then stir with a wooden spoon until a dough begins to form.

Knead the dough with the dough hook (see Notes) on medium speed until a smooth but slightly sticky dough forms, 6 to 8 minutes. If the dough is sticking to the sides of the mixer bowl, add 1 to 2 tablespoons more flour and knead for another 1 to 2 minutes, until the dough doesn't stick to the bowl.

Transfer the dough to a large well-oiled bowl and cover with plastic wrap or a clean kitchen towel. Let the dough rise in a warm spot until doubled in size, 30 to 60 minutes. Meanwhile, grease a 9-by-13-inch (22 by 33 cm) baking pan with butter.

Make the filling: In a small bowl, mix together the brown sugar, softened butter, and cinnamon until well combined.

Once the dough has doubled in size, turn it out onto a clean, well-floured work surface and roll it out into a 12-by-18-inch (30 by 45 cm) rectangle with a lightly floured rolling pin. Spread the filling all over the dough.

recipe continues

For the glaze

2 cups (240 g) powdered sugar

¼ cup (60 ml) strong brewed coffee or espresso (see Notes)

¼ cup (60 ml) heavy cream

2 teaspoons pure vanilla extract

With a long side of the dough rectangle facing you, roll the dough into a tight log. Use a bread knife or unflavored dental floss (see Note) to cut the log crosswise into 12 equal rolls about 1½ inches (4 cm) wide. Arrange the rolls in the greased pan in four rows of three. Cover the dish tightly with plastic wrap and let the rolls rise until puffy, another hour or so.

NOTE: If using dental floss to cut your rolls, slide the floss underneath the roll of dough, cross the ends over the top, and pull tight.

Preheat the oven to 350°F (180°C).

Once the rolls have puffed up, warm the heavy cream in the microwave until it's just slightly warm, 20 to 30 seconds (or warm it in a small pan on the stove). Pour the cream evenly over the rolls, then transfer to the oven.

Bake for 25 to 30 minutes, until fully cooked and golden brown. If the rolls are getting too brown after the first 20 minutes, cover the pan loosely with foil and continue to bake. Remove from the oven and let cool slightly before glazing.

Make the glaze: In a medium bowl, whisk together the powdered sugar, coffee, heavy cream, and vanilla. Pour the glaze over the still-warm cinnamon rolls in the pan and serve immediately.

Store in an airtight container in the fridge for up to 5 days.

NOTES

- Bread flour gives the cinnamon rolls a better chew and mouthfeel, but if you don't have any you can use all-purpose flour and they'll still turn out great.
- For an extra-strong coffee flavor, dissolve 1 to 2 tablespoons of instant coffee powder in the coffee or espresso before adding it to the glaze.
- If you don't have a stand mixer, turn the dough out onto a lightly floured work surface and knead with your hands for at least 8 minutes to develop the gluten in the dough.
- For thicker cinnamon rolls, cut the log into 9 even pieces and arrange them in a 9-inch (22 cm) square baking pan. They may need a few extra minutes to bake through.

JAMAICAN BLUE MOUNTAIN COFFEE

When it comes to coffee, I didn't know how lucky I was until I left Jamaica and tried to find the beans I grew up on. Coffee grown in Jamaica's Blue Mountains, in the eastern part of the island, is one of the most valued coffees in the world. It all started in 1728 when the then governor of Jamaica brought the first Typica coffee plants to Kingston from the French in Martinique.

The Blue Mountains, with their rich volcanic soil, cool climate, and high elevation, turned out to be the perfect place for growing coffee. Over time, the coffee developed a unique flavor that became famous globally. By the early 1800s, Jamaica was a big name in the coffee trade, and by the 1950s, the Coffee Industry Board of Jamaica was set up to make sure the quality stayed top-notch, using strict rules and standards to protect the reputation of Blue Mountain coffee.

What makes Jamaican Blue Mountain coffee such a standout is the environment where it grows and the care that goes into its production. It's grown at high altitudes, between 3,000 and 5,500 feet (915 and 1,680 m), where the misty climate slows down the growth of the trees. This slow growth process makes the beans denser and brings out more flavor. The rich soil, steady rainfall, and good drainage in this region all add to the coffee's smooth taste, which is known for being mild and without bitterness. It has light floral notes with subtle berry-like acidity and a dried fruit sweetness. Blue Mountain is a clean, elegant, and exceptionally balanced cup of coffee. There's not one singular flavor that sticks out; the more subtle complex profile is what people love about this coffee.

Blue Mountain coffee is also a big part of Jamaica's culture and economy. It's protected by a geographical indication, like Champagne or Parmigiano-Reggiano, which means it must be grown in the Blue Mountains at a specific altitude to earn its name. About 80 percent of Blue Mountain coffee is sold to Japan, so it's not always easy to find. Enjoy it black or with a teaspoon of honey or a splash of rum. Or better still, make a pot, drink half, and use the rest in a batch of Cinnamon Rolls with Sticky Coffee Glaze (page 262) or Rum Cake Tiramisu (page 259).

SEVILLE ORANGE ALMOND CAKE

Serves 8 to 10

Softened butter, for the pan

5 large eggs, separated

¾ cup (150 g) granulated sugar

Grated zest of 1 orange

½ cup (125 ml) fresh orange juice

½ cup (125 ml) extra-virgin olive oil

4 tablespoons (2 ounces/60 g) unsalted butter, melted

1 teaspoon pure vanilla extract

1 teaspoon almond extract

3 cups (385 g) almond flour

2 teaspoons baking powder

½ teaspoon kosher salt

2 tablespoons sliced almonds

¼ cup (60 g) Seville orange (or other bitter orange) marmalade

3 tablespoons powdered sugar

Seville oranges are not native to Jamaica, but they grow all over the island. We use them for medicinal purposes, for making a satisfying lemonade-like drink, and for marmalade. This simple, not-too-sweet cake turns out perfectly every time. You can jazz it up by using dark rum or whiskey with the marmalade instead of water, and you can serve it as is or dressed up with whipped cream and fresh berries on top.

Preheat the oven to 350°F (180°C). Grease a 9-inch (22 cm) springform pan with butter.

In a large bowl, whisk together the egg yolks, granulated sugar, orange zest, orange juice, olive oil, melted butter, vanilla, and almond extract until smooth. Add the almond flour, baking powder, and salt and whisk to form a thick batter.

In a stand mixer fitted with the whisk (or in a bowl with a hand mixer), beat the egg whites on medium speed until they are light and foamy and soft peaks form, 2 to 3 minutes. Transfer the whipped egg whites to the bowl with the batter and gently fold them in with a silicone spatula until incorporated.

Pour the batter into the prepared pan and sprinkle the sliced almonds evenly on the top.

Bake for about 40 minutes, or until the top is golden brown and a toothpick inserted in the center comes out clean. Remove from the oven and brush the orange marmalade on the top of the cake while it's still hot, then let cool.

Once the cake has cooled, in a small bowl, combine the powdered sugar and 1 tablespoon water. Carefully remove the cake from the pan, then drizzle the glaze over the top of the cake. Serve warm.

Store in an airtight container at room temperature for up to 2 days or in the fridge for up to 5 days.

MANGO TANGERINE SORT-OF SORBET

Serves 4

3 cups (420 g) frozen mango chunks (from about 3 large ripe mangos)

6 seedless tangerines, peeled, broken into segments, and frozen for at least 4 hours

¼ to ½ cup (60 to 125 ml) coconut milk

¼ cup (60 ml) honey (optional)

Grated zest and juice of 1 lime

1 teaspoon pure vanilla extract

I call this "sort-of" sorbet because the fruit is frozen and *then* churned, whereas sorbet is churned and then frozen. Both ways are delicious, but this version is much easier to make. The honey in this recipe increases the sugar content, which, along with the coconut milk, leads to a richer, creamier, and more easily scooped sorbet. Sort-of sorbet is great served with Seville Orange Almond Cake (page 267), Tortuga-Style Rum Cake (page 251), fresh fruit, or even a sparkling wine. If you're feeling fancy, leave out the honey and serve a small scoop of sorbet between the starter and main course of your meal as a palate cleanser.

In a food processor or blender, combine the mango, tangerines, ¼ cup (60 ml) of the coconut milk, the honey (if using), lime zest, lime juice, and vanilla and blend until the fruit starts to break up. Scrape the sides of the blender or food processor with a silicone spatula, add a little more of the coconut milk, and blend again until the mixture is smooth and creamy. If it's too thick for your taste, add the remaining coconut milk and blend again. Serve immediately in individual bowls or freeze for an additional 30 to 60 minutes before serving if you prefer a firmer sorbet.

DONUTS *with* STRAWBERRY FILLING

Makes 10 to 12 donuts

One ¼-ounce envelope active dry yeast (2¼ teaspoons)

1 cup (250 ml) whole milk, warmed (see Notes)

¼ cup (50 g) sugar, plus ½ cup (100 g) for coating the donuts

4 tablespoons (2 ounces/60 g) unsalted butter, melted, plus 1 teaspoon butter for greasing

1 tablespoon pure vanilla extract

1 teaspoon kosher salt

½ teaspoon freshly grated nutmeg

2 large eggs, lightly beaten

3½ cups (440 g) all-purpose flour, plus more for dusting

Vegetable oil or other neutral oil, for deep-frying

½ cup (120 g) strawberry jelly (see Notes)

This recipe was inspired by one my favorite Jamaican street foods: jelly donuts, which we buy from street vendors by the box. This is a homemade version of the beloved Prestige Bakery donut, with a hint of nutmeg and a splash of vanilla. These classic yeast-raised treats have a light, airy texture and a delicate crumb. Making them is a process and a true labor of love.

Sprinkle the yeast into a large bowl. Add the milk and whisk to combine. Let sit until the mixture is foamy, about 5 minutes.

Add ¼ cup (50 g) of the sugar and the melted butter, vanilla, salt, nutmeg, and eggs to the yeast mixture and whisk to combine. Add the flour and stir with a wooden spoon until a sticky dough forms. Turn the dough out onto a lightly floured work surface and knead with your hands until the dough is soft and smooth, 4 to 6 minutes. Grease a large bowl with the remaining 1 teaspoon butter and transfer the dough to the bowl, then cover with plastic wrap and let the dough rest until it doubles in size, 45 minutes to 1 hour.

Line a sheet pan with parchment. Once the dough has doubled in size, turn it out onto a lightly floured work surface and use a rolling pin to roll the dough to ½-inch (1 cm) thickness. Cut the dough into 3-inch (7.5 cm) rounds with a cookie cutter or the rim of a drinking glass. If the dough is sticking to the cutter, dip the cutter in flour before cutting again. Knead any scraps of dough together and let it rest for 5 minutes before repeating the rolling and cutting process.

Gently place the cut donuts on the lined sheet pan. You may need to use two trays to ensure each one has at least 2 inches (5 cm) around it. Cover the tray with plastic wrap and let the donuts rise at room temperature (see Notes) until they look soft and puffy, about 1 hour.

recipe continues

Pour 3 inches (7.5 cm) of oil into a large heavy-bottomed saucepan or Dutch oven and heat over medium heat to 350°F (177°C), or until the oil sizzles around a wooden spoon when it's dipped in the hot oil. Line a sheet pan with paper towels and set it near the stove.

Working in batches so you don't overcrowd the pan, gently transfer the donuts to the hot oil and fry until golden, 1½ to 2 minutes on each side. Transfer the cooked donuts to the paper towels to cool slightly.

Pour the remaining ½ cup sugar onto a shallow plate. Place the strawberry jelly in a piping bag.

When the donuts are cool enough to handle, use a paring knife to poke a hole into the center of each donut through the bottom and move the knife from side to side to create a pocket for the jam. Dip both sides of the donuts into the sugar to coat them. Squeeze some jelly into the center of the donuts until the jelly just starts to ooze out.

These donuts are best eaten warm, so enjoy them as soon as they're out of the fryer and filled with jelly.

If you don't manage to eat them all, store leftovers in an airtight container in the fridge for up to 2 days. Reheat them in the microwave until they are just slightly warm.

NOTES

- You can heat the milk in the microwave, or if you don't have a microwave, warm it in a small pan on the stove.
- You can also use strawberry or raspberry jam or even lemon curd instead of strawberry jelly if you wish.
- To make these ahead of time, instead of letting the shaped donuts rise at room temperature, place them in the fridge to rise overnight, then fry them in the morning to have fresh donuts for breakfast.

THE DONUT MAN

Rush hour in Kingston traffic is a lot. It's hot, it's noisy, and the drivers are incredibly creative. Stoplights are chaotic and often gridlocked. Car horns honk impatiently. There are three guys who all want to wash your windshield, while another guy is asking for money. There's someone selling tiny bags of peanuts on the other side of the intersection. And then, like a bell in a storm, you hear it: "Donut, donut! Prestige donut!" It's the donut man and he's walking toward your car with a dozen red and white boxes of sugary goodness. These are Prestige donuts, baked in a heavily secured, nondescript building in downtown Kingston with a faded sign and a bus stop out front. You can buy them in a box of six or eight, but never just one. And honestly, it's nearly impossible to eat just one anyway.

Despite their lack of marketing or a website or social media, you can always find Prestige donuts. They are everywhere in Jamaica, and whether you're walking or driving or even riding in a bus, there's a donut man somewhere nearby hawking this sweet treat.

CHEWY ORANGE GINGER COOKIES

Makes 18 to 20 cookies

8 tablespoons (4 ounces/115 g) unsalted butter, at room temperature

¾ cup (165 g) packed dark brown sugar

1 large egg

¼ cup (60 ml) molasses

1 tablespoon pure vanilla extract

1 tablespoon grated fresh ginger (see Note)

Grated zest of 1 orange

2 cups (250 g) all-purpose flour

1 teaspoon baking soda

1 teaspoon ground cinnamon

½ teaspoon kosher salt

¼ teaspoon freshly grated nutmeg

¼ cup (50 g) granulated sugar

These orange ginger cookies are all about the chewy texture and bright flavors. Fresh ginger and orange zest add a zing that cuts through the sweetness, while molasses gives each bite a rich, deep undertone.

In a stand mixer fitted with the paddle (or in a large bowl with a hand mixer), beat the softened butter and brown sugar on high speed until light and fluffy, 3 to 4 minutes (or longer with a hand mixer). Scrape down the sides of the bowl with a silicone spatula, then add the egg, molasses, vanilla, ginger, and orange zest and mix on high speed until well combined, about 3 minutes.

Place the flour, baking soda, cinnamon, salt, and nutmeg in a medium bowl and whisk to combine. Add the flour mixture all at once to the liquid mixture and stir with a silicone spatula until just combined. Cover the bowl with plastic wrap and place it in the fridge for 30 minutes to let the dough firm up slightly before baking.

While the dough is in the fridge, preheat the oven to 350°F (180°C). Line two sheet pans with parchment paper.

Place the granulated sugar in a shallow bowl or plate. Once the dough has chilled, use a portion scoop or a tablespoon to scoop small balls of dough the size of a golf ball—you'll need about 2 tablespoons of cookie dough for each ball. Roll the balls of cookie dough in the sugar and place them on the parchment-lined sheet pans about 2 inches (5 cm) apart. Use your fingers to flatten the balls slightly.

Bake for 10 to 12 minutes (use the top and middle racks if your pans won't fit side by side), until the cookies are golden brown around the edges, rotating the pans front to back halfway through. Let cool fully before serving. Leftovers will keep in an airtight container at room temperature for up to 5 days.

NOTE: You can substitute 2 teaspoons ground ginger for the fresh ginger, but mix it in with the flour.

COCONUT MAGIC PIE

Makes one 9-inch (23 cm) pie

For the crust

2 cups (250 g) all-purpose flour

2 tablespoons granulated sugar

1 teaspoon kosher salt

¼ teaspoon freshly grated nutmeg

8 tablespoons (4 ounces/115 g) cold unsalted butter, cubed

¼ cup (60 ml) ice-cold water

For the coconut filling

4 egg yolks

¼ cup (30 g) cornstarch

One 14-ounce (400 ml) can coconut milk (1¾ cups)

1 cup (250 ml) heavy whipping cream or whole milk

½ cup (100 g) granulated sugar

2 tablespoons (1 ounce/30 g) unsalted butter

2 tablespoons coconut rum or dark rum (optional)

2 teaspoons pure vanilla extract

2 teaspoons coconut extract

½ teaspoon kosher salt

1 cup (100 g) sweetened shredded coconut

ingredients continue

Pie isn't a particularly Jamaican dessert, but coconut and rum—two of my favorite tastes of home—happen to go perfectly together in a buttery crust. In this creamy, coconutty pie, getting the filling just right is key—you want it silky, not runny, with the perfect balance of coconut flavor and just enough rum to make things interesting. You will need a dose of patience for whisking and watching until the filling thickens to a luscious, pudding-like consistency. The result is smooth and rich, and with a hint of rum, it's a little bit of magic in your mouth.

Make the crust: In a medium bowl, combine the flour, granulated sugar, salt, and nutmeg and whisk to combine. Add the cubed butter and use your fingers or a fork to work the butter into the flour until the mixture resembles coarse crumbs. Slowly add the water and knead gently with your hands to form a firm dough—it shouldn't be crumbly at this stage—being careful not to overwork the dough or the pastry won't be flaky. Form the dough into a ball and wrap it with plastic wrap. Let it rest in the fridge for at least 30 minutes.

Using a rolling pin and working on a lightly floured work surface, roll the chilled pastry dough into a round ¼ inch (6 mm) thick. Transfer the rolled dough to a 9-inch (23 cm) pie pan and gently work it into the pan, being careful not to stretch the dough too much. Pinch the edges of the dough together with your fingers along the edges of the pie pan and then trim any excess crust with a sharp knife. Refrigerate the pie dough for 20 minutes.

Meanwhile, preheat the oven to 375°F (190°C).

Once the pie dough has chilled, place a piece of parchment paper loosely over the dough in the pan and fill the pan with pie weights or dried beans. Make sure to push some of the weights or beans to the sides of the pie shell so it doesn't shrink during baking.

recipe continues

For the topping

1½ cups (375 ml) cold heavy whipping cream

3 tablespoons powdered sugar

2 tablespoons coconut rum or dark rum (optional)

1 teaspoon pure vanilla extract

½ cup (45 g) unsweetened coconut flakes, lightly toasted (see Note, page 55)

Bake for 12 to 15 minutes, until the edges of the crust start to brown gently and firm up. Remove the pie crust from the oven and carefully remove the parchment paper and pie weights or dried beans. Poke holes all over the bottom of the crust with a fork or a small knife, then return the pie crust to the oven and bake another 15 minutes, until fully cooked and golden brown. Remove from the oven and let cool fully.

Make the coconut filling: In a medium bowl, whisk together the egg yolks and cornstarch until smooth. Set near the stove.

In a medium saucepan, stir together the coconut milk, heavy whipping cream, and granulated sugar. Cook over medium-high heat until the mixture just starts to simmer, then slowly pour about ½ cup (125 ml) of the hot mixture into the bowl with the egg yolks and cornstarch while whisking to temper the eggs. Pour the egg mixture into the saucepan with the liquids and whisk together. Reduce the heat to medium and cook, stirring constantly, until the mixture starts to thicken and bubble, 4 to 5 minutes. Make sure to scrape the bottom of the saucepan with a silicone spatula so the bottom doesn't burn. Continue to cook, stirring constantly, until the mixture is as thick as pudding, another 3 to 4 minutes.

Add the butter and stir until it melts, then add the rum (if using), vanilla, coconut extract, and salt and stir to combine. Strain the mixture through a fine-mesh sieve into a bowl big enough to fit the filling. Stir in the shredded coconut. Pour the coconut filling into the cooled pie crust and place a piece of plastic wrap on the surface, gently smoothing out the filling with your hands. Refrigerate until the filling is cold and thickened, at least 3 hours or overnight.

Make the topping: In a stand mixer fitted with the whisk (or in a bowl with a hand mixer), combine the cream, powdered sugar, rum (if using), and vanilla. Whisk on medium-high speed until stiff peaks form, 4 to 5 minutes.

Spread the whipped cream on top of the coconut filling and top with toasted coconut. Serve immediately.

Store in an airtight container in the fridge for up to 4 days.

COOL IT DOWN

DRINKS

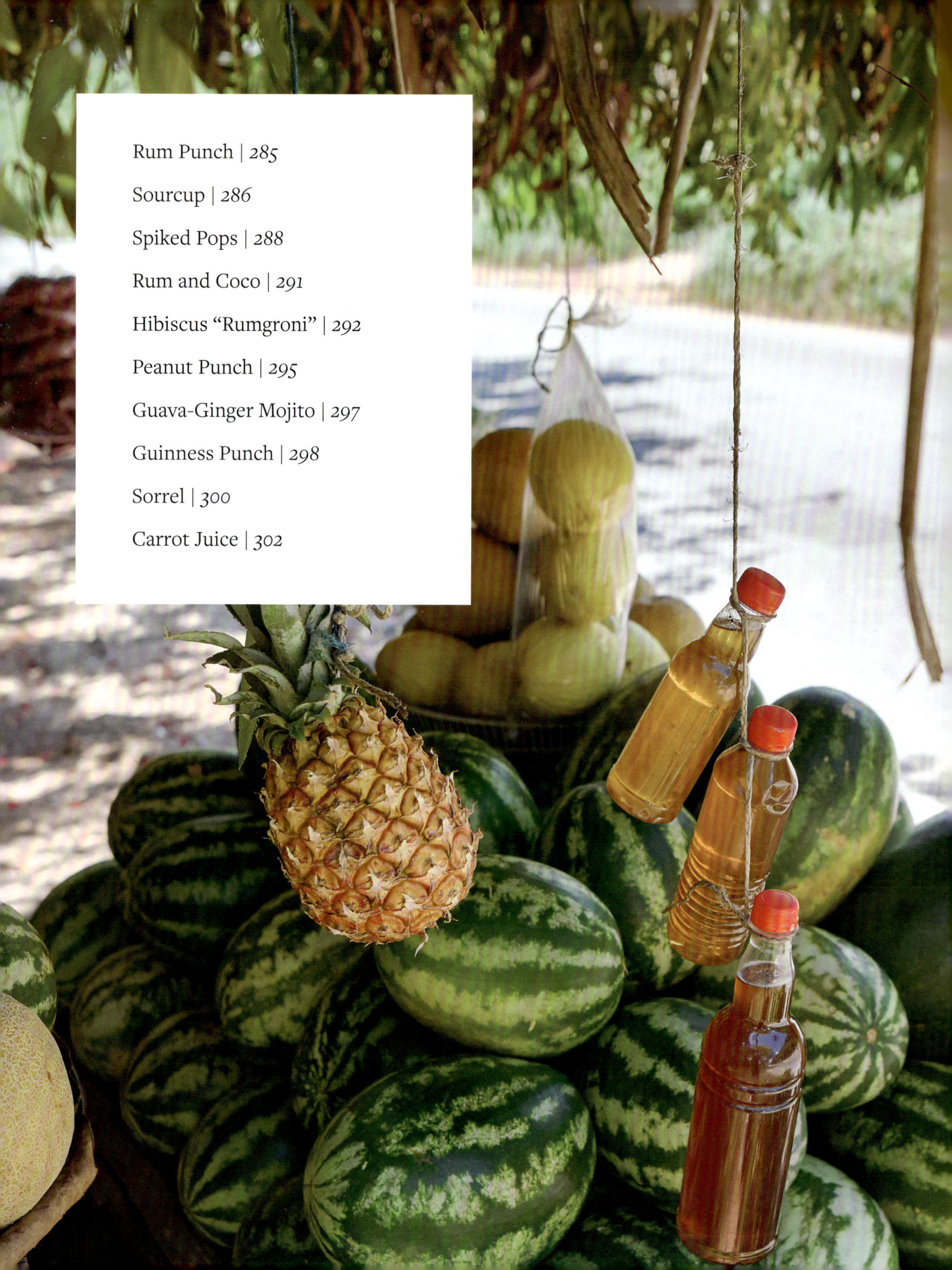

The smell of stale beer mingles with ganja smoke in the tiny bar. Country music blares from worn-out speakers, the guitar twang fitting somehow perfectly with the rhythm of clinking glasses and dominoes slamming onto a table. A woman behind the bar pulls a flask of overproof rum from the cabinet and plonks it next to four ice-filled plastic cups and two bottles of Ting. Laughter punctuates the air as she hands a Red Stripe to a nearly toothless old Rasta seated at the bar.

This is the rum bar, and it's a huge part of Jamaican culture. In fact, it's been said Jamaica has more rum bars per square mile than any country in the world. And it's no wonder—the history of rum is the history of the island itself. Rum was born as a by-product of the sugar industry, which was powered by the labor of enslaved Africans and their descendants. Imbibing was a way to ease some of the hardships of slavery, temporarily at least.

You won't find a Hibiscus "Rumgroni" or a Sourcup at a rum bar, but it is here that we gather, share, and connect.

RUM PUNCH

Makes 6 servings

2 cups (500 ml) pineapple juice

2 cups (500 ml) orange juice

1 cup (250 ml) dark rum, preferably Appleton Estate

1 cup (250 ml) white rum, preferably Wray & Nephew

½ cup (125 ml) fresh lime juice

½ cup (125 ml) grenadine syrup

½ cup (100 g) cane sugar

Ice

Ancient Romans mixed wine with water, herbs, and spices. A drink similar to punch was brought to Europe from India in the 1600s using five key ingredients: alcohol, sugar, lemon, water, and spices. Rum punch is said to have been crafted by British sailors who mixed their rum rations with sugar, citrus, and spices to make the rum more palatable. We don't have to make rum palatable anymore, but we do like to dress it up with juices and syrups to make it bright and refreshing. If you find it too strong, just reduce the amount of rum or add more ice.

In a large pitcher, combine the pineapple juice, orange juice, dark rum, white rum, lime juice, grenadine, and cane sugar. Stir well to dissolve the sugar. Serve in glasses over ice. Leftovers will keep for up to 1 week if stored in the fridge without ice.

SOURCUP

Makes 1 cocktail

2 ounces (60 ml) soursop juice

2 ounces (60 ml) dark rum, preferably Appleton Estate 12

½ to 1 ounce (15 to 30 ml) fresh lime juice

½ ounce (15 ml) Thyme-Allspice Syrup (recipe follows)

½ ounce (15 ml) egg white or aquafaba (optional)

Ice

1 dried orange slice, for garnish

Don't be deterred by the name—this drink is not sour. The star of this cocktail is the soursop, a tropical fruit with spiky, dark-green skin and a soft, juicy pulp inside. Its taste is often described as a blend of sweet and tangy, with hints of strawberry, pineapple, and citrus, along with a creamy mouthfeel, a little like banana. The allspice and thyme syrup brings warmth and balance to this delicate cocktail.

In a cocktail shaker, combine the soursop juice, rum, lime juice, thyme-allspice syrup, and egg white (if using). Shake vigorously for 30 seconds to 1 minute. Add ice and shake again until well chilled, another 30 seconds or so. Strain into a coupe glass without ice and garnish with a slice of dried orange. Serve immediately.

Thyme-Allspice Syrup

Makes about 1½ cups (375 ml)

1 cup (200 g) sugar

1 teaspoon whole allspice berries

8 thyme sprigs

In a small saucepan, combine 1 cup (250 ml) water, the sugar, allspice berries, and thyme sprigs. Bring to a boil over high heat, then reduce the heat to medium and simmer for 5 minutes to allow the flavors to infuse. Cool before using in cocktails. Leftovers will keep in the fridge in an airtight container for 1 month.

SPIKED POPS

Makes 15 to 20 or more depending on the bag size

4 cups (1 L) fruit juice (see Variations)

1 cup (250 ml) dark rum or spirit of choice

This recipe is a nod to a favorite childhood refreshment, the Suck Suck: frozen juice in a bag. Spiked pops, as the name implies, are the grown-up version. Just cut off a corner (or an end, depending on the shape of the bag) and suck out the frozen juice. If you're ever in Jamaica at Carnival, truckloads of slightly frozen rum and juice in a bag are tossed into the gyrating crowds as they dance their way through the streets of Kingston. Spiked pops are a party in a bag.

In a pitcher or bowl, combine the fruit juice and rum and mix well. Pour into ice pop bags or an ice pop mold and freeze until solid. Serve frozen. Leftovers will keep in the freezer for up to 1 month.

VARIATIONS

Mango Pineapple Spiked Pops: Mix 2 cups (500 ml) mango juice with 2 cups (500 ml) pineapple juice.

Mango Passion Fruit Spiked Pops: Mix 2 cups (500 ml) mango juice with 2 cups (500 ml) passion fruit juice

Guava Strawberry Spiked Pops: Mix 3 cups (750 ml) guava juice with 1 cup (250 ml) strawberry juice. Or blend 3 cups (750 ml) guava juice with 1 cup (220 g) frozen strawberries.

Coconut Lychee Spiked Pops: Mix 1 cup (250 ml) canned coconut milk with 3 cups (750 ml) lychee juice.

SUCK SUCK

Suck Suck—the ice-cold refresher of my childhood—is also known as sky juice, bag juice, coolings, serve-me-long, suck a bag (in Trinidad), and suck-a-bubbies (in Barbados). This brightly colored, frozen sweet drink comes in a rainbow of colors. When I was young, the red always sold out first. You can find vendors everywhere: outside school gates, at major stoplights, and on half of the handcarts downtown.

Mama Cherry made Suck Suck for us in the summertime, and sometimes even sold the icy treats to other kids in the neighborhood. The ingredients are simple: some kind fruit-flavored beverage with lots of sugar and lime juice, or syrup and lime juice, and dye—bright red, yellow, neon green, blue. We never asked for cherry flavor or banana flavor—we picked our poison by color. Suck Suck is like a snow cone, but in a plastic bag. You bite a small hole into a corner of the bag and suck out the semi-frozen drink.

Suck Suck is cheap to make, constantly in demand, and provides huge returns, so it's no wonder there are so many Suck Suck manufacturers in Jamaica, some making the juice under questionable conditions. The government of Jamaica eventually stepped in and tried to get all the manufacturers to adhere to the Processed Food Act, which covers things like food safety practices. But Jamaica is a little bit Wild West, and I doubt the day will ever come when you can't find an unmarked Suck Suck.

RUM AND COCO

Makes 1 cocktail

Ice

2 ounces (60 ml) dark rum, preferably Appleton Estate 12 (see Note)

1 ounce (30 ml) coconut milk

1 ounce (30 ml) Coconut Syrup (recipe follows)

½ ounce (15 ml) fresh lime juice

Lime wedge, for garnish

Some things just belong together—Mac and Cheese (page 138), Ackee and Saltfish (page 78), and rum and coconut. But not plain old coconut water (though that also goes well with rum and is a healthier option) and not just regular coconut milk from a can. No, this is a coconut milk cocktail all dressed up for a night on the town.

In an ice-filled cocktail shaker, combine the rum, coconut milk, coconut syrup, and lime juice and shake until well chilled, about 30 seconds. Strain into an ice-filled rocks glass and garnish with a wedge of lime.

NOTE: If you can't find Appleton Estate 12 dark rum, you could use something like Mount Gay XO from Barbados or Flor de Caña 12 from Nicaragua, which are both fruity but somewhat on the dry side.

Coconut Syrup

Makes about 1¾ cups (400 ml)

One 14-ounce (400 ml) can coconut milk (1¾ cups)

1¾ cups (350 g) sugar

1 teaspoon pure vanilla extract

¼ teaspoon kosher salt

In a small saucepan, combine the coconut milk, sugar, vanilla, and salt and cook over low heat, stirring constantly, until the sugar dissolves, about 5 minutes. Let cool before using in a cocktail. Store in an airtight container in the fridge for up to 1 month.

HIBISCUS "RUMGRONI"

Makes 1 cocktail

Ice

1 ounce (30 ml) dark rum

1 ounce (30 ml) Campari

1 ounce (30 ml) sweet vermouth

½ ounce (15 ml) Hibiscus Syrup (recipe follows)

Orange peel, for garnish

If you like Negronis, this is the tropical version. The hibiscus syrup adds a floral sweetness that plays off the deep caramel and molasses notes of the rum. Sweet vermouth brings a smooth, rich depth, while Campari offers its signature bitter edge, creating a perfectly balanced drink. The orange peel garnish adds a bright, citrusy aroma to every sip, rounding out the flavors with a hint of zest. It's bold, complex, and definitely sexy.

In an ice-filled cocktail shaker, combine the rum, Campari, vermouth, and hibiscus syrup. Stir to combine, then strain over a large ice cube into a rocks glass. Garnish with a twist of orange peel.

Hibiscus Syrup

Makes about 2 cups (500 ml)

1 cup (30 g) dried hibiscus flowers (see Note)

1 cup (200 g) granulated sugar

½ cup (110 g) light brown sugar or cane sugar

In a small saucepan, combine 2 cups (500 ml) water, the hibiscus flowers, granulated sugar, and brown sugar. Bring to a boil over high heat, then reduce the heat to low and simmer until the flowers soften and the sugar has dissolved, about 10 minutes. Remove from the heat and let cool completely, then strain the syrup through a fine-mesh sieve, pressing the hibiscus to extract as much syrup as possible. Transfer to an airtight container and store in the fridge for up to 1 month.

NOTE: If you can get fresh hibiscus flowers, use ½ pound (225 g) of them in place of the dried hibiscus in this recipe.

THE MANY SHADES OF RUM

What's your go-to rum—white, amber, or maybe something dark and mysterious? Maybe you've heard that darker means better? Not quite. Turns out, color doesn't tell you much at all. In fact, all rum starts out as clear, so-called "white" rum. The color of rum, from palest gold to deepest pecan, comes from barrel aging or additives like caramel or molasses. But some rums are aged and then filtered to look clear. Some are not aged at all but look dark thanks to additives. Others are blends of light and dark rums from different islands entirely. So if color's not the clue to a rum's flavor, what is? Knowing a little bit about how and where a rum was made will give you a better idea of what to expect when it hits your taste buds. To start with, about 90% of the world's rum is made by distilling fermented molasses. Rum made this way tends to be rich and full-bodied, sweet and smooth. Rum made from freshly squeezed sugarcane juice, on the other hand, has a grassy, fresh taste with vegetal notes. In the French Caribbean this rare style of rum is called rhum agricole. How a rum is distilled matters too. Pot distillation—the way rum has been made for centuries—makes heavier, more intensely flavored rums. Pot stills, common in Jamaican, Guyana, and Barbados, produce small batches of rum with big personality. Column stills, more common in Spanish-speaking countries, make lighter, less intensely flavored rums in a continuous process. Take J. Wray & Nephew, Don Q Cristal, and Clément Blanc: three white rums, but wildly different flavors. J. Wray is bold and fiery, a punchy molasses-based Jamaican overproof, perfect for rum punch. Don Q Cristal, a Puerto Rican rum, is clean and crisp, distilled multiple times, aged in oak, and charcoal-filtered for clarity and softness—more like vodka in a mojito than your typical rum. And finally, Clément Blanc, a grassy, fresh rhum agricole from Martinique. To drink it like a local, make a Ti' Punch: squeeze a little fresh lime into a glass, add cane syrup and unaged rhum, and stir. No ice, unless you must. The bottom line? You can't judge a rum by its color.

PEANUT PUNCH

Serves 2

1½ cups (375 ml) oat milk (or substitute your preferred milk)

1 cup (150 g) unsalted dry-roasted peanuts

½ cup (125 ml) sweetened condensed milk

½ cup (125 ml) water

1 teaspoon pure vanilla extract

½ teaspoon freshly grated nutmeg

½ teaspoon ground cinnamon

Pinch of kosher salt

2 ounces (60 ml) white rum (optional)

Ice

Peanuts are high in protein, low in carbs, and full of good healthy fiber. Peanut punch is a beloved Jamaican drink that blurs the line between beverage and meal. While many modern recipes lean on peanut butter, I start with roasted peanuts for a deeper, toastier flavor. Blend them smooth with oat milk, condensed milk, and a touch of spice—and don't be shy with the nutmeg. Some people spike their punch with Guinness Stout or white rum, but it's just as satisfying alcohol-free.

In a blender, combine the oat milk, peanuts, condensed milk, water, vanilla, nutmeg, cinnamon, and salt and blend until smooth and creamy. Stir in the rum (if using). Serve over ice.

GUAVA-GINGER MOJITO

Makes 1

Leaves from 2 mojito mint or spearmint sprigs, plus more for garnish

½ ounce (15 ml) Ginger Syrup (recipe follows)

2 to 3 ounces (60 to 90 ml) guava juice or puree

2 ounces (60 ml) white rum, preferably Havana Club 3 (see Note)

1 ounce (30 ml) fresh lime juice

Ice

Club soda or sparkling water, to finish

The classic Cuban mojito perfectly illustrates how the right rum can elevate a simple drink. I use Havana Club 3 for mojitos, to pay tribute to Cuba's traditional methods of rum-making. It is citrusy with a hint of oak from its time in bourbon barrels. This guava-ginger mojito is a twist on the classic mojito—just a quick stir, and it's ready to enjoy.

Place the mint leaves and ginger syrup in a highball glass and use a cocktail muddler or a wooden spoon to gently crush the mint leaves. Add the guava juice, white rum, lime juice, and some ice and stir to combine. Top with a splash of club soda and garnish with more mint leaves.

NOTE: If you can't get Havana Club 3 white rum, Don Q Cristal also works.

Ginger Syrup

Makes about 1¼ cups (310 ml))

1 cup (200 g) cane sugar or light brown sugar

½ cup (50 g) washed and smashed fresh ginger

In a small saucepan, combine 1 cup (250 ml) water, the sugar, and the ginger and bring to a boil over high heat. Reduce the heat to low and simmer for 10 to 15 minutes, until the syrup is gingery enough for you. Let cool, then strain through a fine-mesh sieve. Transfer to an airtight container and store in the fridge for up to 1 month.

GUINNESS PUNCH

Serves 2 or 3

One 12-ounce (354 ml) bottle Guinness Extra Stout, cold

1 cup (250 ml) cashew milk or almond milk (or substitute your preferred milk)

⅓ cup (80 ml) sweetened condensed milk

½ cup (40 g) quick or rolled oats

1 teaspoon pure vanilla extract

½ teaspoon freshly grated nutmeg

½ teaspoon ground cinnamon

Pinch of kosher salt

Ice

This is first and foremost a grown-up smoothie, but leave out the alcohol and it can be a family-friendly, breakfastworthy punch. Oats are among the most nutrient-dense foods you can eat. Just throw everything into a blender and voilà!

In a blender, combine the Guinness, cashew milk, condensed milk, oats, vanilla, nutmeg, cinnamon, and salt and blend on high speed until smooth. Pour over ice and serve immediately. Leftovers (without ice) will keep in an airtight container in the fridge for up to 5 days.

SORREL

Serves 12

3 cups (90 g) dried hibiscus flowers, or 1 pound (450 g) fresh

2 cups (400 g) cane sugar

1 cup (100 g) sliced peeled fresh ginger, crushed

1 teaspoon allspice berries

¼ teaspoon whole cloves

2 cinnamon sticks

Peel of 1 orange

Ice (optional)

This refreshing, ruby-red drink is most often served at Christmastime in Jamaica. The taste of the sorrel itself is a little like a floral, lemony cranberry, but for Christmas we warm it up with cloves, ginger, allspice, and, depending on the company, rum.

In a large saucepan, combine 12 cups (2.8 L) water, the hibiscus, sugar, ginger, allspice berries, cloves, cinnamon sticks, and orange peel. Bring to a boil over high heat, then reduce the heat to low and simmer for 15 minutes. Turn off the heat and let it sit on the stove overnight to allow the flavors to develop further.

Strain through a fine-mesh sieve or a cheesecloth, then transfer to a pitcher or other large container. Store in an airtight container in the fridge for up to 2 weeks. Serve cold or over ice.

SORREL = CHRISTMAS

If you're lucky enough to spend Christmas in Jamaica, you have no doubt tried sorrel. The ruby-red libation served on ice is as much a part of the holiday as twinkling lights or the heady aroma of a rum-soaked Christmas pudding (page 248) baking in the oven.

This flowering tropical shrub is a member of the mallow family, making it cousins with cacao, okra, cotton, and durian, to name a few. It's a species of the beautiful flowering hibiscus you see in so many ads for Hawaii and the Caribbean. *Hibiscus sabdariffa*—sorrel's scientific name—is also known as roselle, red sorrel, Jamaican sorrel, and Florida cranberry, among others. Whatever you call it, sorrel didn't originate in Jamaica. It is believed to have been brought to the island by enslaved Africans, like so many of our other traditional plants and foods. It took root in the island's fertile soil and became a beloved part of our food heritage.

Most parts of the sorrel plant are edible or useful in some way. The leaves are eaten as a vegetable in some tropical and subtropical countries, like a spicy spinach. The flowers, a smaller version of the flowering hibiscus, are also edible. The calyx, which is the external part of the flower, is its most versatile feature. On the plant, the calyx is a striking crimson red and has a smooth, fleshy texture. It can be used for flavoring, coloring, and making teas. The calyx is also used in making wine, jam, juice, jelly, and syrup and sometimes as a spice. A type of hemp can be extracted from the stems to create a strong fiber for making twine, sacks, and cords. Sorrel is a good source of calcium, iron, magnesium, antioxidants, and vitamin C. It has been used to treat colds and poor circulation and to relieve a hangover. Tea made from the calyx is said to be effective in lowering blood pressure.

As a chef, I've used sorrel to create infused sauces, sorbet, and even glazes for meats. Sorrel jelly, made from the same steeped liquid as the drink, pairs beautifully with meats—especially ham or roast chicken. In Jamaica, sorrel is best known for making a refreshing, tart beverage spiced with ginger, cloves, and allspice berries that is often finished with a healthy splash of rum—because what's Christmas in Jamaica without a little rum?

CARROT JUICE

Serves 6

2 pounds (900 g) carrots, peeled and chopped

One 14-ounce (400 ml) can sweetened condensed milk

1 teaspoon pure vanilla extract

½ teaspoon grated fresh ginger

½ teaspoon freshly grated nutmeg

½ teaspoon ground cinnamon

Pinch of kosher salt

Ice

This creamy, sweet, delicately flavored nectar of the gods will make you think of carrot juice in a whole new way. Make sure you get good-quality, fresh young carrots for this drink. If the carrots are at all bitter, that taste may come through. If you wish, you can swap out the carrots in this recipe for calabaza squash or Jamaican pumpkin.

In a blender, combine the carrots and 5 cups (1.2 L) water and blend on high speed until smooth, about 1 minute. Strain the carrot juice through a cheesecloth or press through a very fine-mesh sieve. Rinse the blender jar, then pour the strained carrot juice back into the blender.

Add the condensed milk, vanilla, fresh ginger, nutmeg, cinnamon, and salt and blend until smooth, about 30 seconds. Pour over ice and serve immediately. Leftover carrot juice will keep in an airtight container in the fridge for up to 1 week.

FROM SCRATCH

FLAVOR FOUNDATIONS

BAY Leaf
Powder
CLOVES
POWDER
NuT-Meg
PowDe

In Jamaican cooking, the real magic happens long before the first bite. It starts with the seasonings—layers of spice and flavor that bring life to the simplest ingredients. Every culture has its basic flavor palette, and Jamaica is no different. Our base layer comes from what is, and has always been, accessible, affordable, and adaptable. Where other countries use parsley, dill, or oregano, Jamaica holds sacred the trinity of thyme, scallion, and garlic. Together they're used to season almost every kind of meat and soup—usually cooked on a Saturday—and, of course, Rice and Peas (page 127)—usually prepared on a Sunday.

Whether you're making Jerk Marinade for a backyard barbecue or spicing up Fish Tea with the Soup Seasoning, the recipes in this chapter will guide you through the bold, vibrant flavors that define Jamaican food. These are the same seasonings I grew up watching Mama Cherry use, and now it's my turn to pass them on to you.

GREEN SEASONING

Makes about 3 cups (750 ml)

6 scallions

1 bunch of parsley, stems included

1 medium onion, chopped

Cloves from 1 garlic head (about 12 cloves), peeled

½ cup (125 ml) vegetable oil, other neutral oil, or extra-virgin olive oil

¼ cup (25 g) thyme leaves (about 12 sprigs)

½ green bell pepper, seeded

1 Scotch bonnet pepper, seeded

1 tablespoon chopped fresh ginger

1 tablespoon kosher salt

Grated zest and juice of 1 lime

1 tablespoon distilled white vinegar

½ teaspoon ground allspice

At home we call this *blen-up* (as in "blend-up"). Green seasoning is the backbone of many traditional dishes and great for marinating meats, seasoning roasted vegetables, or adding depth to stews and soups. The ingredients in the herb-packed mix vary from island to island, and even from kitchen to kitchen. Most Jamaicans typically use whatever leftover herbs they have on hand—that little piece of onion at the bottom of the fridge, the scallion you didn't use up last night, the three sprigs of aging thyme that have started to shed their tiny leaves.

This bright, bold blend is easy to make and keeps well in the fridge, so you can always have a fresh burst of flavor on hand.

In a blender or food processor, combine the scallions, parsley, onion, garlic, oil, thyme, bell pepper, Scotch bonnet, ginger, salt, lime zest, lime juice, vinegar, and allspice. Blend until smooth, then transfer to a mason jar or airtight container. This green seasoning will keep in the fridge for up to 1 month in an airtight container.

ESCOVITCH PICKLE

Makes 1 quart (roughly 1 L)

- 1 cup (250 ml) distilled white vinegar
- 2 tablespoons sugar
- 2 teaspoons kosher salt
- 1 teaspoon allspice berries
- 1 thyme sprig
- 2 Scotch bonnet peppers, cut into thin strips
- 1 large carrot, cut into thin strips
- 1 small red bell pepper, cut into thin strips
- 1 medium yellow onion, thinly sliced

This spicy pickle is a vinegar-based condiment, influenced by Spanish escabeche (from when Spaniards colonized Jamaica). It breathes life into any fried seafood.

In a medium saucepan, combine ½ cup (125 ml) water with the vinegar, the sugar, salt, allspice berries, and thyme. Bring to a boil over medium-high heat, then add the Scotch bonnets, carrot, bell pepper, and onion. Reduce the heat to low and simmer until the vegetables start to soften slightly, 3 to 5 minutes. Let cool. Once cooled, the pickle can be stored in an airtight container in the fridge for up to 1 month.

SCOTCH BONNET SAUCE

Makes 1 quart (roughly 1 L)

1 cup (190 g) diced pineapple, fresh or canned

6 Scotch bonnet peppers, halved (see Notes)

5 garlic cloves, smashed and peeled

1 medium carrot, diced

1 yellow onion, diced

1 tablespoon grated fresh ginger

½ cup (125 ml) distilled white vinegar

3 tablespoons sugar

1 tablespoon kosher salt

1 teaspoon ground cumin

½ teaspoon ground turmeric

Everything is better with hot sauce, at least if you're Jamaican. Having a good hot sauce recipe in your back pocket is a gift. This one offers bright citrus notes, just the right amount of heat, and the perfect pitch of sweet. Use it wherever you want your food to get a kick of flavorful heat.

In a medium saucepan, combine the pineapple, Scotch bonnets, garlic, carrot, onion, ginger, and 3 cups (750 ml) water. Bring to a boil over high heat, then reduce the heat to maintain a simmer and cook until the vegetables are tender, 10 to 15 minutes. Remove from the heat and let cool.

Transfer the cooled mixture to a blender and add the vinegar, sugar, salt, cumin, and turmeric. Blend on high speed until smooth. If the sauce seems too thick, add a little more water to reach a pourable consistency. Store in an airtight jar or bottle in the fridge for up to 1 month.

NOTES

- For a milder hot sauce, remove the seeds from the Scotch bonnet peppers before adding them to the recipe.
- If you can't find Scotch bonnet peppers, substitute habanero peppers in this recipe.

SOUP SEASONING

Makes about 1 cup (200 g)

- 3 tablespoons all-purpose or rice flour
- 3 tablespoons garlic powder
- 3 tablespoons onion powder
- 2 tablespoons kosher salt
- 1 tablespoon ground turmeric
- 1 tablespoon dried parsley
- 1 tablespoon dried thyme
- 1 tablespoon paprika
- 1 teaspoon freshly ground black pepper
- 1 teaspoon chili powder or dried Scotch bonnet pepper flakes (optional)

Like many Jamaicans, I relied for many years on the convenience of powdered soup mixes—including the ubiquitous Grace "Cock Soup" mix (whether spicy or regular)—because every cook knows the secret to a satisfying dish is in the seasoning. You can make your own soup blend with nuanced flavors using store-bought herbs, spices, and aromatics. This homemade mix transforms a simple pot of soup into a culinary masterpiece.

In an airtight container or screw-top jar, combine the flour, garlic powder, onion powder, salt, turmeric, parsley, thyme, paprika, black pepper, and chili powder (if using). Shake well. The mixture will last up to 6 months if kept in an airtight container in a cool, dark place.

GRACE COCK SOUP

Soup Saturday is a longstanding tradition for many Jamaicans, and a good soup seasoning is key. Grace Cock Soup Mix is a staple in most Jamaican households. It adds depth to soups and stews or is used to season fish and chicken dinners. Its versatility makes it an indispensable part of Jamaican home cooking, offering a quick and flavorful shortcut for building complex, rich dishes. With a name that raises eyebrows outside the Caribbean, this mix doesn't actually contain chicken but is packed with herbs and spices that bring any soup (especially chicken soup) to life, imparting a mild, savory flavor with a hint of heat from Scotch bonnet peppers. If you don't have time to make the Soup Seasoning (recipe above) and you're not concerned about the derision and hilarity if your friends see the name on the box, Grace Cock Soup Mix is a great option.

Escovitch Pickle
Scotch Bonnet Sauce
All-Purpose Seasoning
Scotch Bonnet Mayo
Mango Chutney

Dry Jerk Rub
Soup Seasoning
Jerk Marinade
Jerk Mayo
Green Seasoning

ALL-PURPOSE SEASONING

Makes about 1 cup (200 g)

¼ cup (60 g) kosher salt

3 tablespoons garlic powder

3 tablespoons onion powder

3 tablespoons paprika

2 tablespoons dried thyme

1 tablespoon freshly ground black pepper

1 tablespoon dried oregano

1 tablespoon dried parsley

1 tablespoon sugar

1 teaspoon cayenne pepper

1 teaspoon ground turmeric

1 teaspoon ground allspice

As the name suggests, this Swiss knife of the seasoning drawer works with almost anything. Put it on meats, seafood, soups, stews, and roasted vegetables and they will taste better.

In a small bowl, whisk together the salt, garlic powder, onion powder, paprika, thyme, black pepper, oregano, parsley, sugar, cayenne, turmeric, and allspice. The seasoning will keep for up to 3 months when stored in a mason jar or other airtight container.

JERK MARINADE

Makes 1 quart (roughly 1 L)

¼ cup (60 ml) distilled white vinegar

¼ cup (60 ml) soy sauce

10 garlic cloves, peeled

Leaves from 12 thyme sprigs (about 3 tablespoons)

6 scallions, chopped

3 or 4 Scotch bonnet peppers (see Note)

1 medium yellow onion, chopped

2 tablespoons molasses or light brown sugar

2 tablespoons minced fresh ginger

2 tablespoons vegetable, canola, or extra-virgin olive oil

2 tablespoons allspice berries

2 tablespoons kosher salt, plus more to taste

1 tablespoon freshly ground black pepper

1 tablespoon chicken bouillon paste

1 teaspoon ground cinnamon

1 teaspoon freshly grated nutmeg

Grated zest and juice of 1 lime

This is an excellent marinade for chicken, pork, or beef and is also the base for Jerk Mayo (page 319), which makes for a killer sandwich topping. The marinade is a great flavor enhancer for proteins and vegetables, with the best results on the grill, as the smokiness complements the flavors in the marinade.

In a blender or food processor, combine the vinegar, soy sauce, garlic cloves, thyme, scallions, Scotch bonnets, onion, molasses, ginger, oil, allspice berries, salt, black pepper, bouillon paste, cinnamon, nutmeg, lime zest, and lime juice. Pulse until well combined and mostly smooth. Season to taste with more salt. Store the marinade in an airtight container in the fridge for up to 1 month.

NOTE: For a milder jerk paste, use fewer Scotch bonnet peppers, or remove the seeds from the peppers before blending the jerk marinade. If you can't find fresh Scotch bonnet peppers, you can use habanero peppers instead.

PIMENTO, AKA ALLSPICE

The pimento we use so much in Jamaican cooking comes from the dried berries of the *Pimenta dioica* tree. Also called allspice because it smells like cinnamon, cloves, and nutmeg, Jamaican pimento is known for its high oil content, making it the finest quality in the world. The trees are indigenous to Jamaica and were once plentiful all around the island. Increasing demand for pimento by-products (essential oils, leaves for cooking, wood for smoking) has led to unsustainable harvesting practices and all four species of the plant found in Jamaica are under threat.

A lot of Jamaican pimento is now grown on farms, which improves consistency but also makes it more expensive: It takes 5 or 6 years for a pimento tree to start producing berries, and at its full fruit-bearing capacity (20 years) a tree will still produce only 10 to 20 pounds (4.5 to 9 kg) of pimento berries per year. If you also consider that the berries need to be picked at exactly the right time—when they've reached their full size but while they're still green (they lose their aroma if allowed to ripen fully)—you start to get an appreciation for the cost of producing allspice. Once harvested, the berries are spread out on a flat concrete area (called a barbecue) to dry in the sun for 4 to 5 days, where they turn a deep reddish brown.

DRY JERK RUB

Makes about 1 cup (150 g)

- ¼ cup (60 g) kosher salt
- 3 tablespoons onion powder
- 3 tablespoons garlic powder
- 1 to 2 tablespoons dried Scotch bonnet pepper flakes (see Note)
- 2 tablespoons dried thyme
- 2 tablespoons ground allspice
- 2 tablespoons freshly ground black pepper
- 1 tablespoon brown sugar
- 1 tablespoon ground ginger
- 2 teaspoons smoked paprika
- 2 teaspoons dried parsley
- 2 teaspoons chile flakes
- ½ teaspoon freshly grated nutmeg

This is the dry version of the jerk marinade. It is more accessible and versatile in that you can put it on fries, on plantain, or in your salsa or use it to season your meats. You could even go wild and put it on your popcorn.

In a bowl, stir together the salt, onion powder, garlic powder, Scotch bonnet flakes, thyme, allspice, black pepper, brown sugar, ginger, smoked paprika, parsley, chile flakes, and nutmeg. Store in an airtight container at room temperature for up to 3 months.

NOTE: If you can't find dried Scotch bonnet pepper flakes, you can substitute the same amount of cayenne pepper.

MANGO CHUTNEY

Makes about 2 cups (650 g)

- 1 tablespoon vegetable oil or other neutral oil
- 1 shallot, minced
- 1 garlic clove, minced
- 1 tablespoon minced fresh ginger
- ½ teaspoon ground cumin
- ¼ teaspoon chile flakes
- ¼ teaspoon ground turmeric
- ¼ teaspoon ground allspice
- 3 large mangoes, chopped, or 3 cups (500 g) frozen mango chunks
- ½ cup (110 g) packed brown sugar
- ¼ cup (60 ml) apple cider vinegar
- 1 teaspoon kosher salt

This is one of my favorite condiments. It has the perfect balance of sweetness from the mango and tangy/tart from the vinegar and just the right amount of spice. Mango chutney goes with just about anything: in a sandwich or—my favorite—with any kind of curry. This recipe is best with fresh mangoes, but frozen will do if you can't find any.

Heat the oil in a medium saucepan over medium heat. Add the shallot, garlic, and ginger and cook until fragrant, about 1 minute, stirring occasionally. Add the cumin, chile flakes, turmeric, and allspice and stir for another minute or so.

Add ¼ cup (60 ml) water and the mango, brown sugar, vinegar, and salt. Bring to a boil, then reduce the heat to medium-low and cook the mixture until syrupy, 15 to 20 minutes.

If you prefer a smoother chutney, pulse the mixture in a food processor or blender until you reach the desired consistency. Transfer the chutney to a mason jar and let cool. Leftover chutney will keep in the fridge for up to 1 month.

SCOTCH BONNET MAYO

Makes about ½ cup (120 g)

½ cup (110 g) mayonnaise

2 garlic cloves, minced

1 teaspoon Scotch Bonnet Sauce (page 310)

1 teaspoon capers, chopped

Grated zest and juice of 1 lime

This will be your new favorite condiment. It makes for an unforgettable sandwich or wrap topping, or add a dollop on your boiled eggs at breakfast. Tired of your same old blue cheese dip for wings? Use this instead.

In a small bowl, stir together the mayonnaise, garlic, Scotch bonnet sauce, capers, lime zest, and lime juice. Store in an airtight container in the fridge for up to 2 weeks.

JERK MAYO

Makes ¼ cup (60 g)

¼ cup (60 g) mayonnaise

1 tablespoon jerk marinade, homemade (page 315) or store-bought

Grated zest and juice of 1 lime

Try jerk mayo as a spread in your sandwiches and wraps, on its own as a dip, or slathered onto corn (page 55).

In a small bowl, mix together the mayonnaise, jerk marinade, lime zest, and lime juice. Store in an airtight container in the fridge for up to 2 weeks.

RESOURCES

For ingredients used frequently in these recipes, I've listed some of my favorite brands, where applicable. Most of these items can be found in the international aisle of many bigger supermarkets or in Caribbean or West African specialty stores. You may also find them on the following websites:

caribshopper.com

jamaicamadeshopping.com

mycaribbeangrocer.com

Ackee (canned): Grace or Linstead Market

All-purpose seasoning: Island Spice or Maggi Season-up!

Bouillon paste or cubes: Better Than Bouillon, Maggi, or Knorr

Browning: Grace

Callaloo: Grace or Linstead Market

Green seasoning: Walkerswood

Jamaican curry powder: Betapac, Grace, or Cool Runnings

Jerk dry rub: Island Spice or Eaton's

Jerk marinade: Walkerswood or Grace

Seville orange marmalade: Walkerswood or Busha Browne's

Soup mix: Grace Cock Soup Mix or Maggi Soup it up!

Tamarind paste: Neera's

Water crackers: Excelsior or National

ACKNOWLEDGMENTS

This book wouldn't exist without a village—and I'm endlessly grateful to mine.

First, to Danya Smith: my project manager, my amazing partner, and the mother of our beautiful son. Your love, patience, and belief in me carried this project from dream to reality. I am endlessly grateful—not only for what you've done but for who you are.

To Corinne Smith, my writer and dear friend—thank you for helping shape these stories into something that feels true to the bone.

To Judy Linden, my agent, who saw the potential in this book before I did. Thank you for always being that voice of encouragement and for your unwavering support throughout this entire process.

To Judy Pray and the incredible team at Artisan—thank you all for believing in this book and bringing it to life with care and creativity.

To Bruce Springsteen and Patti Scialfa—thank you for your encouragement and support along the way. I'll never forget it.

To Michael Condran, my friend and photographer—your photos captured the spirit of every plate and every place. Thank you for your commitment and for your eye for detail.

To Micah Morton, our food stylist; Maeve Sheridan, our prop stylist; and Ashleigh Sarbone, assistant prop stylist and your team—you all made everything shine with your attention to detail and creativity.

To Blue Salt Studio—thank you for the beautiful space.

To all the recipe testers who spent hours testing and tasting and giving feedback—your time and expertise is so appreciated.

To Chef Martin Maginley and Jacqui Sinclair, my mentors, and to Miss Tricia Campbell, my teacher—your guidance still echoes in my kitchen.

To Sean Gonzales, who gave me my first job as a young teen, along with some invaluable professional experiences.

Big thanks to Paul Salmon and Adam Schop of Miss Lily's for believing in me and providing the opportunity and support to kick-start my culinary journey in New York. I value our continued partnership.

To Novia McDonald-Whyte of the Jamaica Observer—thank you for championing Jamaican food and culture every step of the way.

To my peers in New York, Jamaica, and all over the world—thank you for pushing me, inspiring me, and keeping the fire burning.

To Patsy Davis, my mom—thank you for your unconditional love and all the life lessons you've given me.

And finally, to Mama Cherry, my grandmother, who passed before this book became a reality. You are the reason I fell in love with food, the kitchen, and the stories that live inside a good meal. This one's for you.

Respect and gratitude.

INDEX

Note: Page references in *italics* indicate recipe photographs.

D

CHEF ANDRE FOWLES is a Jamaican-born, New York City–based chef and a three-time Food Network *Chopped* champion. Renowned for his bold, contemporary approach to Caribbean cuisine, Andre has been spotlighted by StarChefs New York and featured in *The New York Times*, *Bon Appétit*, *Thrillist*, *VICE*, *Good Morning America*, and the *Today* show. He has also cooked for a long list of celebrities including rock legend Bruce Springsteen.

Andre has hosted multiple dinners at the prestigious James Beard House and participated in leading food festivals across the United States and the Caribbean, including Food & Wine, SOBEWFF, The Family Reunion, and the Jamaica Observer Food Awards.

This is his debut cookbook, created in memory of his beloved grandmother, Mama Cherry, whose love and cooking shaped his life. Her legacy lives on in every recipe and fuels his next chapter: returning to where it all began. Andre is launching a breakfast-and-soup restaurant in Kingston, Jamaica, and bringing awareness to his One Pot Foundation, a nonprofit dedicated to improving food access and nutritional education for children across the island.